To: Laura Geiger
With lots of love

Uncle George Leader

Aug 6, 1985

Acknowledgements

I would like to express my deepest appreciation to the following persons, without whom I could not have written this book: to Governor George Leader and all the people who graciously consented to be interviewed so I could obtain much of the information for this book; the Bureau of Archives and History of the Pennsylvania Historical and Museum Commission which provided invaluable assistance in obtaining the written record of the Leader Administration; and to my co-author for his perspective, insight, and cooperation. Finally, a special note of thanks is due to everyone who gave me support and assistance in the preparation and completion of the manuscript, my editor and publisher, and to Dr. Sigmund Smith, Teresa Schuhart, Gwen Kennedy, and most especially my wife, Magdalena Cooper.

Richard J. Cooper

Governor George M. Leader

THE POLITICS
OF PROGRESS

By
Richard J. Cooper
and
Ryland W. Crary

PENNS VALLEY PUBLISHERS
Harrisburg, Pennsylvania
1982

Published by Penns Valley Publishers
1298 South 28th Street, Harrisburg, PA 17111
Copyright © 1982 by Penns Valley Publishers
All rights reserved
Printed and bound in the United States of America

Library of Congress Cataloging in Publication Data

Cooper, Richard J.; Crary, Ryland W.
   The politics of progress.

   Includes index.
   1. Leader, George M., 1918-   . 2. Pennsylvania —
Politics and government — 1951-   . 3. Pennsylvania —
Executive departments — Reorganization. I. Crary,
Ryland Wesley, 1913-   . II. Title.
JK3625 1981.C66   353.974807'3'0924   81-21068
ISBN 0-931992-42-7   AACR2

All photos used herein were supplied by and are used with the permission of
the Bureau of Archives, Pennsylvania Historical and Museum Commission,
Harrisburg, Pennsylvania.

Preface

Pundits enjoy rating former state governors, as well as ex-presidents of the United States, on scales ranging from "great," "near great," "average," "mediocre," to "failure," or from "good" to "bad," or from "effective" to "ineffective." While such ratings are at best highly subjective, their accuracy and usefulness depend upon the availability of authoritative documentation and publications. Lamentably, as governors come and go in rapid succession, their performances seldom receive the scholarly attention required for objective evaluation.

Pennsylvania has only a few such evaluations of its forty-four governors who have served since 1790. And of those governors, none has been given more scholarly attention than George M. Leader (1955–1959), who could serve but one term by then existing constitutional provisions. Such attention was due in large measure to the Governor's strong sense of history and his heavy reliance upon university and college personnel resources.

As noted on page 14, this publication is the fourth of a series of scholarly studies dealing with the Leader administration. While there is some overlapping, this volume differs in tone and substance by its concentration on the many innovative policies and programs that were launched and have remained fundamentally intact. I know of no study that demonstrates more clearly how a young governor, against great odds, successfully marshalled what personal, political, and managerial skills were at hand to establish a record which ranks him among Pennsylvania's best chief executives.

John H. Ferguson, Professor Emeritus of
Political Science and Public Administration,
The Pennsylvania State University

v

Table of Contents

Introduction

A book such as this, about a man who was governor of Pennsylvania over 20 years ago is interesting and valuable not only from a historical point of view, but because it reveals what is possible in American government. All too frequently one hears disparaging remarks about "all politicians" and resignation to the inevitability of corruption and/or inefficiency. This is unfortunate because, as this book will show, decent, progressive, honest and efficient government is possible when we elect good people to office. An administration such as Governor Leader's is rather rare in American politics, and, especially in Pennsylvania politics, simply because not enough effort is put into selecting good officials.

The unexpected election of a youthful, vigorous and bright person in the face of a numerically stronger opposition party brought to office an idealistic and well educated man who made every effort to improve the government for the people of Pennsylvania. His efforts were not always popular or successful, frequently because they were misunderstood, but they were honest and more importantly they were needed.

In many ways Governor Leader's administration can be compared to that of President Kennedy. Both were young, idealistic and vigorous in their pursuit of liberal reform. Both called on and relied heavily upon the expertise of the academic community. Both were controversial and made enemies among established politicians, but most of the changes they made have persisted, and have improved the lives of many.

Leader firmly believed that the government was created for the citizens, not the citizens for the government. This simple distinction has far reaching implications. Leader thought that government existed to help those who could not help themselves. This humanitarian tendency surfaced in a number of programs during the Leader administration. The most notable of the humanitarian programs were the mandatory special education legislation, reform of the Department of Welfare and the mental health system, increased benefits for the unemployed, and safety regulation enforcement.

Leader personally felt responsible as governor for the well-being of the less privileged, and he did all in his power to effect improvement in the plight of those dependent upon the state for survival.

Conservation of human and natural resources was based on former Governor Pinchot's concept of "use without abuse." Leader believed that future generations should be able to have as fine a quality of life or better than the present generation. His concern for human resources was even stronger and was reflected in many of his administration's programs: such as the higher education plan, the state park program, and mental health treatment.

Leader rejected the traditional political way of handling problems and programs in the state. He leaned toward techniques employed by public administration rather than the more popular political techniques. Three aspects of public administration were emphasized during the Leader administration: the implementation of sound business procedures, the professionalization of staff, and the use of research for decision making.

George Leader firmly believed in the old adage "you are only as good as the people around you." An examination of state government in subsequent administrations shows that Leader had chosen good people because many of them continued in their jobs or returned later, to work for other governors.

What follows is the story of Governor Leader and the people he brought into his administration; and, how their idealism and expertise impacted on a conservative and politicized state government. It shows how elected officials can make drastic improvements in government when they have the integrity and will to try.

Leader was born on January 17, 1918, to Guy A. Leader and the former Beulah Boyer. His Pennsylvania Dutch family had farmed land in York County for many generations. He attributed to that ancestry his logical way of thinking and his stubbornness. Raised on a farm, he had a Jeffersonian affection for common people and nature. He was always proud of his agrarian background and drew on it for problem solving and inspiration. He personified the Protestant work ethic and made frequent reference to Pennsylvania Dutch sayings. A favorite observation of his was "to Pennsylvania Dutch farmers it is a sin to expect any success without hard work; they have a healthy disrespect for any accidental fertility of the soil."

The third of seven children, Leader came from a family where Christian virtues were valued along with hard work. His early schooling was in a one-room school house, for which he retained high esteem. Afterwards, he attended York High School. Although his father did not have the opportunity of going to college, he wanted his children to do so, and most of them did. George attended Gettysburg College for three years, where he focused on political science, philosophy, and economics. His last year of college was spent at the University of Pennsylvania, preparing to become a teacher. He graduated from there in 1939.

During the same year, he married Mary Jane Strickler. They had four children: Michael, Frederick, Jane Ellen, and David, who was born while Leader was governor.

Both Leader and his wife entered graduate school at the University of Pennsylvania in 1942. Her application stated she aspired to learn more about government in order to aid her husband's political career. Among his professors was Dr. James Charlesworth, who later became a trusted advisor during and after his gubernatorial campaign. His graduate courses had great influence on Leader's ideas about government generally and particularly public administration.

Graduate study was interrupted after one semester by the Second World War. Leader became an ensign in the Navy for three years, and served as a supply officer on the aircraft carrier U.S.S. Randolph. Afterwards, he attributed to that naval training and experience some of his administrative capabilities. When the war ended, he returned to Pennsylvania and poultry farming with his father.

Leader launched his political career in 1942 as secretary for the York County Democratic Committee, becoming chairman in 1946. While he served in that capacity, his father was elected to a seat in the state senate left vacant in 1943 by the death of Henry Lanius, a blind senator from York. Guy Leader remained in the Senate for only one full term, after

4

finishing a partial term. He left feeling disappointed because of Republican dominance.

George Leader followed in his father's footsteps in 1949, when he ran for the state senate and won. Four years were spent in that body, where he was regarded as a good senator by his peers and constituents. He read pending bills avidly and became known as a junior senator who kept himself informed on issues. A liberal democrat, he voted for the controversial Fair Employment Practice Bill, which failed of passage until his term as governor. He voted also against the Pechan Act, inspired by the anti-communist campaign launched nationally by United States Senator Joseph McCarthy, which required loyalty oaths of candidates for, and holders of, state and local offices in Pennsylvania.

George Leader ran unsuccessfully in 1952 for the elective office of State Treasurer. Although defeated, he considered the effort worthwhile inasmuch as it provided invaluable experience in conducting a statewide campaign and established his name with the public.

No governor is elected in a vacuum. Rather, economic, social, and political circumstances shape both direction and outcomes. A recession or natural disaster, for example, can make or break a governor.

Long-term trends also have important bearings upon what happens politically. Pennsylvania is illustrative: After World War I, population and economic growth declined relative to other states; its mighty industrial strength weakened; the number of farmers dropped steadily; huge rail investments ended in bankruptcy; coal and oil industries lost their former supremacy; and the depression of the 1930s left many parts of Pennsylvania chronically depressed.

Politically, it was during the 1930s that Pennsylvania ceased being the Republican stronghold it had been since the Civil War. Governor Pinchot, a Progressive Republican, led the way with elections in 1922 and 1930. Then followed the triumphs of Democrats nationally, the election of a Democrat —Earle—as Governor, in 1936, and increasing Democratic strength in large cities and depressed areas. The four Republican governors who succeeded Earle—James, Martin, Duff, and Fine—left controversial war and post-war legacies which fostered Democratic confidence and resurgence. It was that set of circumstances which made possible the election of Governor George Leader.

Realistic Democrats did not expect to win the 1954 gubernatorial election. Only once in this century—in 1936, had the Democrats won that high office, and Richardson Dilworth, former Mayor of Philadelphia, was the candidate preferred by most Democratic leaders. When Dilworth withdrew, because he thought the chances of winning were too slim, Leader was viewed more favorably. He was first considered for Lieutenant Governor, but when his name was suggested for Governor, he decided to seek the nomination. In the eyes of many Democratic leaders, he was a respectable token candidate to offer as a sacrifice to a seemingly inevitable Republican triumph.

Leader, however, did not expect to lose. He watched the Democratic party grow in York County and was confident that an address to the crucial issues would sway voters. Whether it was the issues or the manner of the young, energetic candidate who outshown his opponent, especially on television, was not measurable, but Leader's victory came as a surprise to most observers. The party supported his candidacy, even though he had not been its first choice.

Leader was 36 years of age at the time, and bubbling with both idealism and energy. He believed he had a tradition to uphold, not of inflexible political dogmas, but of the ideals of Pennsylvania's founder, William Penn. He quoted often this statement of Penn's inscribed on a Capitol wall:

> There may be room there for such a Holy Experiment, for the nations want a precedent and my God will make it the seed of a nation. That an example may be set to the nations, that we may do the things that are truly wise and just.

Frequent references were also made to Penn's broad humanitarianism and what may have been his greatest contribution —religious toleration. It was those high goals which Leader set for himself.

6

Governor Leader and Pittsburgh Mayor David L. Lawrence.

Chapter 1

The Governor and His Office

THE ROLE OF GOVERNOR

A governor's role is one which only a small number of individuals ever learn or have the opportunity to act out. That role must be learned, either by experience, trial and error, or by consulting with people familiar with a state's operations.

The activities of a governor can be classified into three general categories: ceremonial, political, and managerial. Those tasks, especially in large states, have become so extensive that no one can perform them without much help from many sources. Today's governors have sizeable staffs, budgets, and bureaucratic establishments. The political party usually provides backup support. Each governor has his or her own style, preferences and priorities, which almost certainly become evident soon after inauguration.

The ceremonial responsibilities are many and varied. The governor is chief of state—the official representative of the public. As such, invitations pour in to throw out the first balls at games, welcome conventioneers, attend county fairs, dedicate new facilities, and similar ceremonial activities. Proclamations are issued declaring days, weeks, and months for every conceivable event. Egg Month, Blind Week, Driver Safety Week, and Secretary Day are but a few examples. After election, the governors appear to rise, in a way, above party politics. Whether people voted for or against him or her, many of them take pride in having the governor attend their meetings, champion their causes, or show interest in them in other ways.

The political activities of a governor depend largely upon his or her inclinations and tastes. Some prefer to be a party figurehead; others relish being the actual leader. In either case, the governor usually is looked upon as the party standard-bearer throughout the state and nation. Typically, the governor controls state patronage, with party assistance. Although the number of patronage jobs has diminished in most states, enough remain to provide governors with both a source of power and headaches as well.

A governor's relationships with the legislature are of primary importance. Each governor's style and approach differs somewhat, but routinely interaction centers around such matters as sponsoring bills, nominating persons for whom legislative approval is required, threatening or using the veto, submitting and justifying budgets, and conferring endlessly with individual legislators or groups of them. Some governors have power enough to dominate the legislative process, but even in those situations, negotiations and compromises between conflicting views and interests are common. Some governors work well with legislators regardless of political affiliation and get most of what they want while others feud endlessly and get little.

As chief executives, governors have extensive managerial duties inasmuch as they must oversee the entire executive establishment, except possibly for a few agencies which have been given a high degree of independence by constitution or statute. A governor can take an active or passive role in management; in either case a bureaucracy of considerable size and specialization stands ready to assist, or possibly obstruct, leadership and direction. Since state administrative structure is pyramidical and hierarchical in form, the governor's contacts usually are limited to heads of departments and agencies, although exceptions are numerous. A governor must also deal with serious disciplinary cases and crises, including those requiring the use of state national guard contingents.

THE GOVERNOR'S VALUES

Given the roles and duties expected of a governor, one of the most important determinants of how any one person will realize these roles is the values, beliefs and expectations they bring with them to the office.

It is perhaps this realm which distinguishes Governor Leader from so many other governors. While other governors have had strong religious beliefs and values, few have had the courage to stand by them in the face of political and public pressures. The fact that Governor Leader stands out from other governors reveals an insight into our political institutions and ourselves. It is always easier to compromise—or just do nothing—when opposed by powerful interests, than it is to fight for what you believe in. This is not an endorsement of the Governor's beliefs, but it is a statement about his character and its importance for understanding his administration.

Governor Leader was a devout Lutheran. He has said, "It is not enough for any of us to be merely against sin; we must be strenuously, ardently for good. Not only should we be endorsers of good, we must be builders of an ever-climbing, always-progressing ladder of morality, into new, hitherto impossible heights. Christian virtue has no final step." Christianity guided his daily life; he even spoke at Sunday services about the applicability of Christian principles to all aspects of life, including government. Leader was convinced that the only way to have good government was to follow the teachings of Jesus Christ, and he repeatedly compared the work of government officials to the work of true Christians. He once said, "it is my overwhelming belief that our system of government is but an extension of Christianity."

His Christianity was not dogmatic; he was an extremist about virtue, but not about doctrine. Leader was tolerant and accepted all religious beliefs. Speaking on religious freedom for the Amish he said, "Sometimes I believe we forget that there is no standard mold which makes human beings Americans." As long as a person was virtuous and true to his faith, he had Leader's support. An example of Leader's relig-

10

ious tolerance is seen in his close connection with the Jewish faith. Leader frequently spoke at benefits that raised bonds for Israel. These efforts culminated in a trip to Israel and the dedication of the green belt in Jerusalem, of which the Leader Woodland is a part. At the planting of the trees ceremony, Leader and his wife planted the trees on their hands and knees, instead of ceremonially breaking the earth with a shovel.

To George Leader, a promise was a moral obligation. This belief shocked some of his political contemporaries, who failed to persuade him that campaign promises were merely tools to get elected. Leader realized many of his campaign promises, and the one notable exception is also an example of his commitment to campaign promises. Leader had pledged to veto any sales tax legislation, but the Republicans were determined to force him to accept the tax. Leader maintained this position as long as possible and the stalemate produced the longest legislative session in Pennsylvania history. Faced with an insoluble impasse and the state's impending bankruptcy, Leader relented and was forced by political pressure to accept the sales tax.

Leader displayed honesty and integrity, as the people who knew him well attest. In a profession which is often shaded by the scandals of political officials lining their pockets at public expense, George Leader stood out as being above reproach. Irregularities occurring during his administration were vigorously pursued and uncovered.

He advocated and saw the passage of a conflict of interest bill in the legislature. Leader's administration was always open to the press; he supported "right to know" legislation which was intended to open governmental records to the press and public. Leader believed that the only way to have government by the people was to have the people fully informed about government activities. A particularly sensitive area for Leader was the influence of special interest groups. He sought legislation that would have required lobbyists to register, enabling the public to know who was influencing whom.

One logical extension of Leader's humanitarian philosophy is found in his efforts to insure human rights for all citizens. He stated directly that "the present administration in Harrisburg is dedicated to people—human values. I believe that all men are brothers under one Father. I believe that governments are the servants of men." Thus, it is not surprising that Leader supported minority groups.

"Minority" was an uncommon term during the 1950's. The idea of the "melting pot" still prevailed and many believed that any group of people who tried hard enough could find their way into the American mainstream. This did not always happen, because prejudices, class stratification, and deep-seated traditions prevented certain races and religions from assimilating freely into American society.

The Fair Employment Practice Council was an example of Leader's dedication to human rights for all citizens. The council, formed in 1956 after about ten years of debate in the Pennsylvania legislature, was not fully accepted even after its creation. Its purpose was to investigate claims of unfair employment practices and discrimination. Leader was convinced that such legislation was overdue and he was happy with its passage. His joy was shortlived, however, because he could not get his nominations for the members of the council confirmed by the Senate. Even after the appointments were confirmed, during the 1957 session, the Republican legislature threatened to reduce the Council's appropriation to a level that would have made it ineffective. The Council later evolved into the powerful Human Relations Commission.

Despite proud historical traditions of tolerance in Pennsylvania, blacks were not accepted fully in society. No black person had ever been a member of a governor's cabinet. Leader was the first governor to select a black person for such a position. He was Andrew Bradley, at first Budget Secretary and later Secretary of Property and Supplies. During Leader's administration, 450 blacks were employed by state government, compared to 98 in the previous administration.

Because of a racial disturbance in Bucks County, Leader formed a committee to investigate fair housing practices, and the Department of Justice created a division of civil rights. When a report issued by the Department of Public Instruction revealed segregation in a Pennsylvania school district, Leader demanded an immediate halt to the practice and ordered that a study be made of all school districts in the

state to determine whether there were other instances of segregation. His administration also sponsored a bill to end
racial discrimination at institutions of higher education in
Pennsylvania.

He regretted that legislation was necessary to remedy
customs which should have ended with feudalism. Leader's
administration supported two bills for women's rights. Far
before his time, and yet in his opinion, long overdue, two bills,
one giving equal pay for equal work and one giving married
women and married men the same rights to sell or mortgage
their property, were supported by Leader in the legislature.

ADMINISTRATIVE STYLE

Early in Leader's administration, Herbert Cohen, Leader's political mentor and Attorney General, advised the Governor that if he wanted to be remembered as a good governor,
he would have to select several key issues or projects and
devote his energies to them, just as Pinchot had stressed
highways and conservation. Although that was conventional
advice, Leader rejected it. He explained that since he had
only four years, he was determined to give the whole job his
best effort. The people had not elected him to be a partial
governor, but to serve the entire state and all of its interests.
George Leader became noted for his concern for all state
departments, agencies, and functions.

As a result of his graduate work in public administration,
Leader was convinced that state government needed *public*
administration not *political* administration. Public administration was a relatively new field in the 1950's. The Fels Institute of Local and State Government was founded in 1937
as part of the Wharton School of Commerce and Finance at
the University of Pennsylvania. The state's chapter of the
American Society for Public Administration was formed as
recently as 1957. Even though political scientists and
philosophers had discussed good-government principles
throughout the centuries, the deliberate training of public administrators, as well as political scientists, was relatively
new. During the 1950's, the major universities and colleges of
the state were preparing people for careers in government at
all levels.

George Leader felt that it was time for the theoreticians to test their principles in the field. At a meeting of the Pennsylvania Chapter of the American Society for Public Administration, held in June, 1957, at Harrisburg, Leader openly invited those present to use Pennsylvania state government as a laboratory, confident that the results could only be an improvement over what preceded. The number of academics found around Harrisburg during the Leader administration made some old-line politicians liken the Capitol to a college campus.

Without a doubt, Leader had more academics working in high places than any of his predecessors. Some critics referred to them as "eggheads" and took a dim view of their roles. Undeterred, Leader's defense was vigorous, claiming "brains" was as important to government as to industry and other walks of life. A generalist himself, he welcomed opposing points of view and was determined to obtain the best qualified personnel available.

The Fels Institute of Local and State Government, headed by Dr. Stephen Sweeney, played a key role in Leader's administration. Shortly after Leader's election, Sweeney suggested that a quick survey be made of departments and other major agencies to determine what changes should be made to improve state government and make its operation more efficient. Such a "pre-inaugural" study would also identify qualified persons and help orient new department and agency heads.* Leader liked the idea and a team of twenty-two members was selected to conduct the surveys. Data was obtained during the month of December and final reports were submitted to the Governor shortly before he took office. Oral presentations were made to each department or agency head about to take office.

---

*Three specialized studies deal with these and related activities: Reed M. Smith: *State Government in Transition: Reforms of the Leader Administration* (Philadelphia: University of Pennsylvania Press, 1963); M. Nelson McGeary: *Pennsylvania Government in Action: Governor Leader's Administration (1955–1959)* (State College, Pa.: Penns Valley Publishers, 1972); and Elias Silverman: *Constraints on Innovation: A Classified Income Tax for Pennsylvania* (unpublished doctoral dissertation on file at the Pattee Library, The Pennsylvania State University).

Research was the cornerstone of Leader's approach to administration. Rather than depending upon the advice of lobbyists, his own opinions, or those of party leaders, he preferred in-depth studies, such as those mentioned above and below. He was particularly fond of using citizens' committees, not only for fact-finding, but also because they provided opportunities for voter participation. That secondary benefit somewhat cushioned the tension between the academics and the politicians.

GOVERNMENTAL DEPARTMENTS AND PERSONNEL

What follows is a survey of most of the departments in Pennsylvania State Government during Leader's administration. An attempt has been made to provide an overview of the various departments, the condition which existed when Leader assumed office, what he and his staff attempted to do within the realm of each department's sphere of influence, and the personnel he selected to help him. Anecdotal accounts of some of the problems and highlights of the governor's term in office also are provided.

Much of Leader's effectiveness was attributable to his reorganization of state government. By restructuring the governor's office, he obtained a staff which could provide professional assistance to him constantly. Thus he developed the capacity to govern not a few but most areas for which he had administrative responsibility.

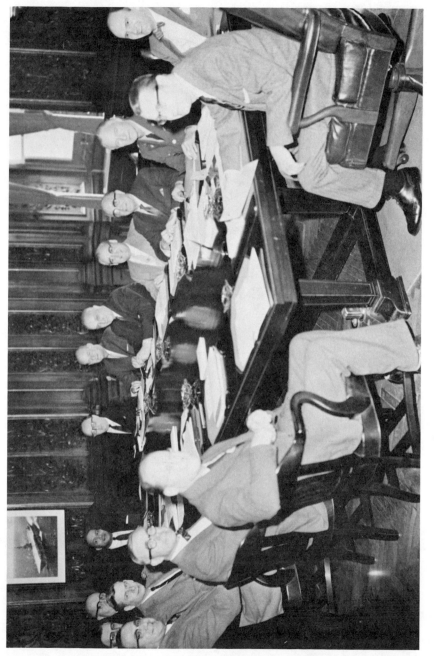

Governor Leader's Cabinet in 1958.

Swearing in Andrew Bradley as Budget Secretary.

Andrew Bradley   Governor Leader   Senator Joseph Barr   James Finnegan

17

Chapter 2

Central Administration

THE GOVERNOR'S OFFICE

One of the most important organizational units in any gubernatorial administration is the office of the Governor itself. Here are ordinarily found diverse groups of individuals working together to enable the Governor to be who he is. Governor Leader's office was no exception; some of the faces were familiar, while others were new, but they endeavored to learn to work together as a team. While the creation of the Office of Administration removed some of the duties and responsibilities from the Governor's Office, that did not diminish its importance. The governor's office staff handled his calendar and correspondence, prepared his speeches, official documents and other ceremonial and political activities.

PERSONAL AIDES

The Governor selected David Randall as his executive secretary. Randall had worked with the Governor throughout his campaign and had run for Congress in 1952 when Leader ran for State Treasurer. Randall explained that he became Leader's executive secretary by accident. After the election, Leader requested Randall to handle the mail while he vacationed in Florida. When Leader returned, he asked Randall to stay on as his secretary. In the reorganization, Randall was placed in charge of that part of the Governor's Office which handled the political and ceremonial activities.

Four operational units fell under Randall's supervision: the offices of the legislative secretary, personnel secretary, press relations secretary, and chief clerk. In addition to serving as one of Leader's aides, Randall was also a political advi-

18

sor. Because of his proximity to the governor, he played a large role in the administration, but unlike department heads, his activities were not associated with one functional area.

Randall's sense of humor kept things light around the Capitol when things looked grim. Many people remembered his technique for guarding the Governor's time. He would come and stand next to the Governor, saying nothing. His silent presence was enough to inform the visitor that the Governor was needed elsewhere.

Otis Morse, a radio and television specialist from York, joined the administration in 1957 as Randall's assistant. He recalled that his first duty was to bring the Governor's correspondence up to date. Morse and Mary Ressler, the Governor's personal secretary, removed the backlog and kept his mail current. When Randall left the Governor's office to enter law school in September of 1958, Morse became Leader's executive secretary. Later he served as Governor Lawrence's executive secretary until accepting the position of Chairman of the Democratic State Committee.

George Leader invited his brother, Henry Leader, a practicing attorney in York, to become Pennsylvania's first legislative secretary. The Governor told Henry that they might succeed or fail, but in any event, the term would not be dull. Leader hoped that the legislators would accept his brother partly because of their father's prior senate experience. Initially, however, many legislators considered the new governor a "governor in short pants" because of his age, and his younger brother a young idealist. But the Leaders were proud of their legislative achievements, stating that despite the difficulties, they were able to get much of the administration's legislative programs enacted.

As legislative secretary, Henry was responsible for coordinating the legislative contacts of the administration, reviewing legislation requested by the departments, and advising the Governor on upcoming bills. Henry briefed the Governor every Sunday evening before those Mondays when the legislature was in session. Because the longest legislative session in Pennsylvania's history occurred during Leader's administration, that meant most Sundays. During the week Henry solicited opinions on bills and needed laws from the executive departments and agencies for use in his Sunday briefings. Employees of the Leader administration remembered Henry best for his insistence upon knowing what needed to be done to improve state government. He would tell them "don't tell me the way something has been done, tell me how it should be done, and we will get it changed."

Another aspect of the Governor's Office, which in previous administrations had more importance, was the Office of Personnel. During Leader's administration that office was directed by Robert "Pop" Jones, a capable politician from Scranton, who had been football coach there for many years. Jones was primarily responsible for patronage appointments. "Pop" had the reputation of being a person who could say "No" and make the listener feel good about it. He did that frequently during Leader's administration, because it was his job to tell county chairmen that available positions had to be filled by qualified candidates before the Bureau of Personnel in the Office of Administration would approve the appointment. In previous administrations, there had been no similar check on patronage hiring.

It was common opinion around the administration that Leader's first choice for press secretary was a mistake. Thomas Hodges, though a capable and talented person, had no press experience. His relationship with the media was poor and the situation rapidly deteriorated. For example, Hodges would order everyone to rise when the Governor entered the room for a press conference, a gesture which the seasoned reporters resented. The Governor finally realized that a new press secretary was needed to improve his relations with the press.

After Hodges resigned, the Governor searched for a new press secretary. Debs Myers, a former editor of *Newsweek* magazine, was recommended by the Democratic National Committee office which knew that Leader was looking for a competent press secretary. Using his extensive journalism background, Myers greatly improved Leader's press relations. Leader lamented that if Myers had been with the administration from the start, things would have been different. To help maintain contact with the citizens of Pennsylvania, Debs Myers started "The Governor's Mail Box," a radio program during which Leader answered questions from letters he had received.

David Baldwin, a speech writer for the administration, was catapulted into the inner circle when Hodges began to falter. As a speech writer, he was closely associated with the press function and remained so when Deb Myers joined the staff. Baldwin was reported to have become so adept at writing Leader's speeches that he could actually anticipate what the Governor wanted to say on any particular occasion. Like the best of secretaries and ghostwriters, he was able to write in the Governor's style of presentation.

George Leader intended to choose a new Chief Clerk for his office, but he was advised that a previous governor had fired Richard Heagy and was forced to reinstate him because of confusion which developed in the Governor's office. Heagy was full of details and knew the proper procedures for every occasion. The new administration found him indispensable. Heagy had served as Chief Clerk since Pinchot's first term. In 1958, George Leader appointed Heagy to his cabinet, as a fitting reward for years of dedicated service. Heagy retired during the Lawrence administration after serving in the Governor's Office for 40 years.

The Chief Clerk was in charge of the E floor, located directly beneath the Governor's Office. Here all the Governor's speeches, press releases, proclamations, and official documents were prepared by the office personnel under the direction of Heagy and Evelyn Pletz, his assistant in charge of word processing.

The establishment of the Office of Administration resulted in overcrowded working conditions in the Governor's Office on the second floor of the Capitol. The Chief Clerk's office was moved to the E floor. This move and the transferral of several functions to the Office of Administration lowered the morale of the Chief Clerk's office. Leader appreciated the dedication of these employees; on several occasions, late at night when they worked overtime to prepare for the next legislative day, the Governor would stop in and thank them personally for their fine work and support.

OFFICE OF ADMINISTRATION

When Leader took office, Pennsylvania state government was comprised of 17 independent boards, commissions, and authorities, and 20 departments, 17 of which were headed by gubernatorial appointees and three (Internal Affairs, Auditor General, and Treasury) were headed by elected officials. No less than 52 officials reported directly to the Governor. To Leader, it was an administrative jungle that no one could govern effectively. To him that state of affairs helped explain the politicization, lack of coordination, inefficiencies, and maverick independence—let alone corruption—which had long been accepted hallmarks of Pennsylvania state government. Both he and his advisors recognized that the time was ripe for drastic reform.

Proposals for reorganizing state government were not new. The State Government Survey Committee, commonly known as the Chesterman Committee, had made an extensive review during the Fine administration, with help from numerous professors of political science and public administration, as well as other specialists. Both Leader and his advisors were aware of the work done by the Chesterman Committee and made considerable use of its recommendations.

At Governor Fine's request, the Pennsylvania Economy League had translated the Chesterman Report into an operative plan for reorganizing the Governor's Office, but it reached him too late for implementation. Fine gave the proposed plan to Leader, who considered it a valuable first step and passed it on to his advisors. Among other provisions, the plan provided for the establishment of an Office of Administration. What emerged later was a somewhat different Office of Administration more to the liking of Leader's advisors, particularly Dr. James Charlesworth, who became its first Secretary.

It was particularly fitting that Charlesworth should become the first Secretary since he had advocated the establishment of such an office for years. His vigorous leadership and broad knowledge got the Office off the ground with neither statutory authorization nor an appropriation. Its legal basis was an executive order, and funds, personnel, and furnishings were given or borrowed from other sectors of the Governor's Office and sympathetic officials. Inasmuch as the Secretary was a personal aide to the Governor, Senate confirmation was not required.

The new Office and its staff were not universally welcomed. Many long-term office holders considered it a threat to traditional prerogatives and ways of doing things. There were, on the other hand, many dedicated officials, including most of Leader-appointed heads of departments and agencies, who welcomed the prospect of reforms which might end abuses, add dignity to public service, and upgrade both benefits and performance.

With the Office of Administration in place, Leader was in a stronger position than his predecessors to administer the executive branch and initiate new programs. Charlesworth was the most visible and probably the most controversial academic. On several occasions, he antagonized some members of the press and politicians with outspoken remarks. Charlesworth was accustomed to making extreme statements as a teaching technique and his style did not change when he became a public official. Leader, however, always supported him, even when he lamented publicly the low-levels of voter education and understanding and proposed tests which would eliminate those who did not measure up to standards.

Charlesworth remained a part of the Leader administration for only a year and a half because of pressing obligations at the University of Pennsylvania and the American Academy of Political and Social Science, of which he was at the time President. Announcing his resignation, Leader said "I regret more than I can say that my good friend, Dr. James Charlesworth, has been forced to make a decision which represents a personal loss to me, and much more important, a public loss to the people of the Commonwealth." Charlesworth was succeeded by Dr. John Ferguson, Professor of Political Science and Director of the Social Science Research Center at The Pennsylvania State University. Dr. Ferguson had been a member of the preinaugural study group and taken leave of absence to become Director of the Bureau of Program Evaluation in the newly established Office of Administration. Ferguson continued the work Charlesworth began and solidified the position of the Office of Administration in state government.

As that Office acquired staff and expertise, its impact was felt on all aspects of state government, including such mundane matters as space allocation, purchasing, expense accounts, and dog-law enforcement. A few other states had moved in similar directions, but in none of them were the consequences in terms of public administration more far-reaching than in politically-charged Pennsylvania.

BUREAU OF ACCOUNTS

The state's accounting system was archaic in 1955. Not one system existed, but several, all of which differed significantly. Changes had been recommended by the Chesterman Committee, but not until the Leader administration was there a concerted effort to implement them.

Besides the lack of uniformity, the major defect was that accounting was done on a single-entry cash basis, with the result that cash balances were available but there was no way of knowing at any given time what receipts and obligations were outstanding. A double-entry accrual system was required to achieve that result. The difference between the two systems can mislead by millions of dollars.

Early in his administration, Governor Leader contracted with the Public Administration Service, headquartered in Chicago, to assist the Office of Administration's Bureau of Accounts in making a study and recommendations. A uniform mandatory system of the accrual type became operative on January 1, 1956, and the first balance sheet ever produced by the Commonwealth was released a year later. The Bureau of Accounts produced a *Manual of Accounting and Related Financial Procedures* as a guide to standardization of the accounting system. Mechanization followed with the installation of high-speed computers, starting with payrolls and extending gradually during the Leader and succeeding administrations to most operations involving massive data processing.

The Bureau of Accounts was first directed by Michael Albers, a Philadelphia lawyer and accountant, who prepared the pre-inaugural study of the Department of Revenue. When he resigned, his replacement was George Cottrell, a Pittsburgh accountant. Cottrell's death prompted the appointment of Elliott Falk, who, as an employee of the Public Administration Service, helped install the new accounting system.

BUREAU OF THE BUDGET

The office of Budget Secretary, established by statute in 1927 as an adjunct to the Governor's Office, became the Bureau of the Budget within the Office of Administration under Governor Leader. That change made the Budget Bureau the only sector of the Office of Administration having statutory authorization. As such, the person heading it had two titles: Budget Secretary and Director of the Bureau of the Budget. To complicate matters further, Governor Leader granted cabinet status to that official.

Andrew Bradley, of Bedford County, was Leader's first designee. Bradley had been one of the first to support Leader for Governor; he had successfully completed his CPA examinations a few months before his appointment. He was at the time Treasurer of the Democratic State Committee, and he had served on the pre-inaugural transition team. Bradley had the distinction of being the first black person of cabinet rank in Pennsylvania.

A law passed during the Fine administration made the comptrollers directly responsible to the Governor through the Budget Secretary instead of the department and agency heads. Leader decided to begin enforcing that previously unimplemented statute. While primary responsibility for enforcement rested with the Budget Secretary, close collaboration with the Bureau of Accounting was required.

Redesigning the comptrollership function was a difficult task, particularly in departments and agencies where full top-level support was lacking. A change of such magnitude required continuous effort to harmonize relationships between the Office of Administration, heads of departments and agencies, comptrollers and their staffs, and among the several comptrollers. A first step was to reduce the number of comptrollers by making each of them responsible for either a single large department or a cluster of smaller departments and agencies; a second step was to upgrade personnel; and a third step was to provide advice, training, and technical support for comptrollers and their staff. Of all of Governor Leader's initiatives, few had a more far-reaching impact on state government than those just mentioned.

The Budget Bureau's major function was fiscal planning, budget preparation, execution and control. That task was exceptionally demanding because budgeting was done on a biennial basis (the change to annual budgets occurred later in the Leader administration), a deficit of $52,293,054 was inherited from the Fine administration, and a deficiency of $39,284,032 had accrued during the fiscal period ending July 1, 1955. Altogether, Leader's budget requests for closing out fiscal 1955-56 came to $1,335,175,561. For the biennium 1957-58, Leader requested $1,439,548,897. The figures mentioned were for the general fund.

Leader's fiscal proposals precipitated a battle royal in the General Assembly where Democrats controlled the House by a slim margin and Republicans controlled the Senate by a similar majority. That stalemate did much to tarnish the Governor's "image" and delay implementation of new programs and administrative reforms. Particularly controversial were Leader's opposition to renewing the sales tax and his counter proposal to enact a uniform classified income tax. Leader preferred a graduated income tax but sidestepped that issue because of doubts over its constitutionality.

The Governor was forced to relent on sales-tax renewal and found little enthusiasm for his classified income tax proposal within or outside the legislature. Moreover, mid-term loss of a Democratic majority in the House, coupled with continuing Republican dominance in the Senate, severely limited Leader's ability to obtain financial backing for both existing programs and new initiatives. Nothing frustrated the young Governor more than the constant haggling over fiscal matters which occurred throughout his administration.

Leader had more latitude in dealing with fiscal administration. Reform of the accounting system was noted above.

Equally far-reaching were steps to modernize budgetary concepts, forms and procedures. Upon entering office, the Governor found the line-item budget in use which detailed expenditures by department, agencies, and objects of expenditure. Preparations began immediately to shift to the program type which focused less on details and more on the lump sums required for program effectiveness. The transition required considerable time. A compromise budget made its appearance for fiscal 1957–58 which took into account the transition to annual budgets as well as the program type. The proposed budget for 1958–59 made further refinements, but it remained for the Lawrence administration to complete the process.

The steps taken by the Leader administration laid the foundation for not only program budgeting but also for a still further refinement during the Shafer administration which installed a Program Planning and Budgeting System (PPBS). The latter system placed heavy emphasis upon program planning, evaluation, and cost-effectiveness, the embryonic origin of which centered in the Bureau of Program Evaluation to which Governor Leader and Secretaries Charlesworth and Ferguson gave top priority. The institutionalization of that evaluative function in the Chief Executive's office was a forerunner of similar steps taken by many other states' government.

Like most of his predecessors, Governor Leader left a sizable deficit for the next governor to reckon with. Secretary Ferguson, who took on the additional tasks of Budget Secretary when Bradley became Secretary of the Department of Property and Supplies, explained the reasons in his final report to the Governor: (1) anticipated operating deficiencies; (2) disappointing tax yields, due chiefly to the economic recession; (3) mandated increases, especially for school subsidies; and (4) rising costs for existing and expanded programs.

BUREAU OF PERSONNEL

When Governor Leader took office there were about 60,000 full-time state employees. Of that total, about twenty percent had civil-service status, most of whom were engaged by the Liquor Control Board and agencies for which such personnel practices were mandated as a condition for receiving federal funds. Union membership was then comparatively small and drawn largely from civil-service ranks.

There was no single centralized agency charged with responsibility for administering personnel functions. Rather, responsibility was spread among the Budget Bureau, the Governor's Personnel Secretary, the Civil Service Commission, and the respective departments and agencies. Governor Leader charged the Office of Administration, through its Bureau of Personnel, with a higher degree of centralized authority than before with the expectation that it would provide the leadership and direction required to attain his objectives. Succeeding governors have centralized personnel management still further.

Governor Leader and many of his Cabinet officers quickly discovered that if existing programs were to be rejuvenated and new ones launched, additional highly competent personnel was indispensable. His first effort was to alert, through the Personnel Secretary, state and county Democratic leaders of not only the state's needs but also their opportunities to supply talent. Some, but not enough, able recruits were obtained. The Governor's second, and unprecedented step, was to persuade the Executive Board to place some ten thousand professional and technical positions under civil service by executive order. The Governor preferred, and strove to achieve, statutory authorization for the purpose but to no avail. Succeeding governors were more successful in gaining legislative support for civil-service expansion.

The Governor did succeed, however, in obtaining numerous qualified recruits, many of whom remained in state employment for long periods of time. Not all were newcomers; rather, many were incumbents who by additional preparation and tests qualified for professional and technical positions placed under civil service. By the end of Leader's term, the percentage of positions covered by civil service had risen from about twenty to forty percent. By early 1981, the percentage had reached about sixty-five.

A second major personnel move was quite revolutionary. There existed at the time Leader took office about 7,000 position classifications which defied rational and equitable administration. Neither time nor staff permitted the technical analysis and reclassification required to modernize the system, so the Governor turned again to the Public Administration Service for assistance. By using questionnaires, interviews, hearings, and analyses, the number of job classifications was reduced to about 1,400, with specifications and pay adjusted correspondingly. Also revamped were policies concerning sick leave, vacations, and other fringe benefits.

A third major undertaking involved the integration of retirement with Social Security. Federal law made that possible and prescribed the standards and procedures to be followed. Getting that gigantic and highly technical task done within prescribed deadlines required a crash joint effort spear-headed by the Office of Administration, representatives of the two retirement boards (one for state employees, the other for public-school employees), the Department of Labor and Industry, the Department of Public Instruction, as well as the respective comptrollers. The Governor's Legislative Secretary, Henry Leader, handled the considerable coordination required with the General Assembly, its staffs, and committees.

As with most of the major projects undertaken through the Office of Administration, shortages of trained manpower impeded action. Never before was so much in-service training undertaken at the state level. The Bureau of Personnel limited its direct training of operating personnel to a few specialized groups, such as clerks, secretaries, and data processors, preferring instead to stress the training of top and middle-management executives who in turn would teach subordinates. A Personnel and Training Council provided a source of leadership and coordination. The Civil Service Commission provided invaluable assistance. So did the Public Service Institute, then a part of the Department of Public Instruction, and professors of political science and public administration from several Pennsylvania universities.

The Bureau of Personnel had three directors: Dr. Gayle Lawrence, Professor of Political Science at Temple University; James Yarger, a private consultant; and Russell Johnson, who had directed the personnel classification and pay project as an employee of the Public Administration Service, and afterwards served as a staff member of the Bureau.

BUREAU OF MANAGEMENT METHODS

Before the Leader administration there was no central specialized agency whose task it was to monitor constantly state government organization and procedures. The Budget Bureau had been attentive to such matters since its establishment in 1927 as it listened to budget requests, appraised financial needs, and special problems were called to its attention. A few departments and agencies, particularly those funded heavily by the federal government, such as the Department of Public Assistance and the Bureau of Employment Security, had competent small staffs for the purpose. Sweeping surveys were made from time to time by special committees or commissions, consultants were occasionally engaged to examine and report on particular departments, agencies, and problems, and legislative committees frequently made inquiries or conducted investigations. Significant as such approaches were, Pennsylvania's sprawling state government was old fashioned, to say the least.

The Office of Administration, led by its Bureau of Management Methods, struck out in all directions but soon was overwhelmed by the magnitude of its task. Counter-part units were established in major departments and agencies to help, and training courses were conducted for deputies, bureau chiefs, and all available management analysis. With the passage of time, a Management Methods Council was organized to lead and coordinate activities of common interest.

Briefed by the pre-inaugural study committee, most heads of departments and agencies responded favorably to the Governor's reform expectations by studying and analyzing their organizations and management systems. Some changes were made promptly; others required considerable time. As new organizational charts and plans made their appearance, they were implemented when approved by the Office of Administration and the Executive Board (a statutory agency made up of the Governor and several department heads).

30

Internal shifts of agencies and functions did not require statutory approval, but inter-agency transfers did. To facilitate action, Governor Leader sponsored and the General Assembly approved legislation, modeled after federal provisions, which permitted inter-agency transfers by reorganization plans as well as by statutes. The use of such plans could sometimes permit quicker action inasmuch as they became effective within sixty days unless disapproved by one or both houses of the General Assembly. Eight such plans were submitted to the legislature during the Leader administration, five of which became effective. That method is still permissible and has since been used from time to time. Internal shifts were numerous and frequent. The successful combination of the Department of Public Assistance and the Department of Welfare was, by comparison, a mammoth undertaking with far-reaching reverberations.

The Bureau addressed itself to numerous other projects, of which the following are illustrative: comptrollership consolidation; payroll mechanization; centralized data processing; uniform expense accounting and control; semi-permanent automobile registration and licensing requiring only the addition of tabs annually; records management and disposal; building-space surveys and allocations; purchasing state automobiles in quantity lots and selling them later at public auction; institutional laundry and food services.

The Bureau's first director was William Austin, on leave from the Atlantic Refining Company and a former federal executive. When he left to become a deputy in the Department of Property and Supplies, he was succeeded by James Greenwood, a former federal executive and management analyst.

BUREAU OF PROGRAM EVALUATION

The reorganization plan prepared by the Pennsylvania Economy League for Governor Fine and later handed to Governor-elect Leader did not include a Bureau of Program Evaluation. That omission was based on the assumption that program evaluation was more properly the function of the Office of Administration as a whole, and particularly the Budget Bureau.

31

Drs. Sweeney and Charlesworth were of the opinion that unless program evaluation was institutionalized separately and strongly supported it would be lost in the shuffle and neglected. Governor Leader accepted that reasoning. Staffing the Bureau proved difficult, and keeping it centered on its major purpose required constant vigilance on the part of both the Governor and the Secretary of Administration.

The Bureau's small staff was supplemented by the resources of other units within the Office of Administration, departments, agencies, consultants, and lay committees appointed for special purposes. An inter-agency council of deputies provided a clearing house for information, leadership, and coordination.

Among the programs given special attention were: the many statistical series then in use; public assistance standards; crime and corrections; schools for veterans' training; Commonwealth publications; older workers; handicapped and retarded children; migrant labor; milk marketing and price setting; professional licensure; school lunch and milk; federal grants-in-aid; school-building design and engineering; mental health; higher education, including community colleges; institutional food services and laundries; labor mediation; and state-owned general hospitals. The conduct of such evaluative studies was interrupted many times by trouble-shooting assignments and calls for assistance from other components of the Office of Administration as well as the Governor himself. Preparatory work for the special commission created by the General Assembly to develop recommendations for constitutional revision was one of such assignments.

Studies such as those mentioned had an important bearing upon all aspects of the work done by the Office of Administration, especially program and capital budgeting, for which priority setting was indispensable. Succeeding administrations preferred not to institutionalize program evaluation separately but to center it in the Budget Bureau, as proposed earlier by the Pennsylvania Economy League. Governor Leader's approach had, however, signalized the critical importance of program evaluation to the art and science of public administration. Whether the Bureau's demise was wise and beneficial is debatable. Critics argue that in the absence of such a bureau, the Office of Administration's role has been reduced to mundane routine controls with little interest in program content and effectiveness.

The Bureau's directors, in the order mentioned, were: Dr. William Seyler, Professor of Political Science at the University of Pittsburgh; Dr. John Ferguson; Dr. Harold Alderfer and Dr. Robert Christie, formerly Professor of History at Lafayette College.

BUREAU OF CAPITAL EXPENDITURES

Prior to the Leader administration, no formal distinction had been made between budgeting for general and special funds and capital expenditures. Rather, as requests for funds came to the Budget Bureau from the several departments and agencies, they included capital items and recommendations as well as others.

The Department of Property and Supplies was the principal line agency concerned with capital plans and projects, but special agencies, such as the General State Authority, School Building Authority, and the State Planning Board (which recently had been transferred to the Governor's Office from the Commerce Department by reorganization plan), were also deeply involved.

Sitting as the Governor did on the boards of special agencies, he was impressed by the need for planning and coordinating building projects costing millions of dollars. It was that concern that led to the establishment of the Bureau of Capital Expenditures in the Office of Administration. Claude Dumars, from Delaware County, was selected to head the Bureau. His experience with such matters was considerable in both federal and private employments.

At first, the Bureau limited its activities to gathering and analyzing the information needed to keep the Secretary of Administration and Governor advised on building activities in progress and contemplated projects. Later, the Bureau became equally involved with capital budgeting and space allocation.

Where capital budgeting was concerned, close collaboration with the Planning Board was required, but obtaining it was difficult because the Board's director was new and had few staff aides. Difficulties were also encountered in determining how roles were to be assigned among other sectors of the Office of Administration, particularly the Bureaus of Budget and Management Methods.

The first capital budget made its appearance in 1958. It was assembled from requests made by departments and agencies with such appraisals, cost estimates, and priorities as the Office of Administration thought appropriate and the Governor approved. The submission of the first capital budget prompted the General Assembly to enact the necessary enabling legislation to make it a permanent feature of state government. Refinements were made by succeeding administrations. Shortly after Governor Leader left office, the Bureau was abolished and its functions were transferred to the Budget Bureau.

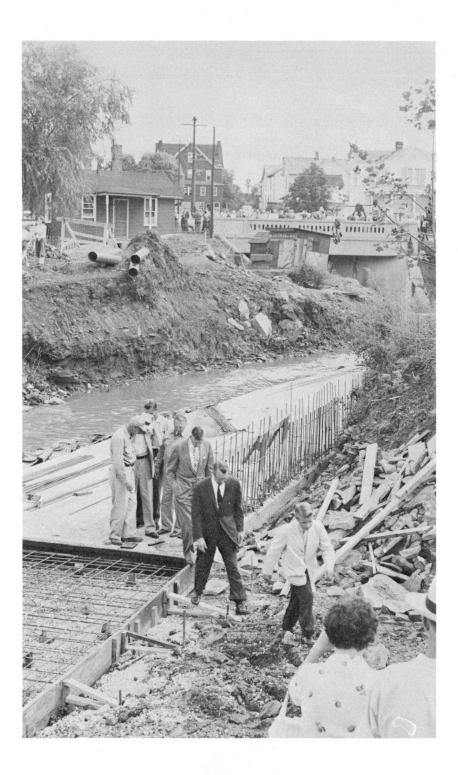

Chapter 3

Human Services

DEPARTMENT OF PUBLIC INSTRUCTION

In perspective, education in Pennsylvania in the 1950's was overdue for many constructive changes. Opportunities for higher education lagged far behind states such as California and Michigan. Although Pennsylvania could boast of several old prestigious colleges, technical institutes, and great universities, community colleges were all but lacking. A true state university system did not exist; and the state teacher colleges were underplanned and underdeveloped.

School building construction did not meet the demand. District reorganization was backward compared with the neighboring states of Ohio, New York, and New Jersey. Despite legislation on the books, special education was tragically primitive. Moreover, curriculum development had grown randomly due to a lack of central leadership. Because state efforts were diverted primarily toward such routine concerns as recordkeeping, the Department of Public Instruction was not a leading force in the state's education.

Governor-elect Leader moved confidently onto the scene. Deeply concerned and knowledgeable about the reality and the need, his objectives were clear, and he moved purposefully. The story of his accomplishment is well known. Education was a high priority for Leader, and his achievements in this area are among his finest administrative attainments.

During his campaign, George Leader accused the Department of Public Instruction of being a fortress of political patronage and he promised to make drastic changes. Not surprisingly, Superintendent Haas resigned on the day of Governor Leader's inauguration. Francis Haas had held the post since 1939 and had gathered together a qualified staff from around the state. Indeed, a position in Harrisburg had been considered a legitimate recognition for administrators who had done well at the local level. However, upon arrival in Harrisburg these same administrators seemed to retreat from initiative and action to mundane tasks. George Leader sensed that there was no real leadership in Harrisburg; he was convinced that the only thing the department did was to keep records. However ably this recording function was exercised, the new governor realized that the Department of Public Instruction should lead education in the state, not just follow it with a record book.

Leader's interest in education was not a surprise to those who knew him. George Leader was very familiar with education in Pennsylvania. Although he had not taught, he studied education in college. As a politician he was aware of education lobbies, and as a concerned father he was aware of the system's operation. It was not by chance, then, that Leader's administration focused a great deal of attention on the state's educational system. In fact, Leader's concern for education went beyond merely academic support. He viewed education as a great humanizing force, and as one of the state's primary concerns.

On assuming office, Governor Leader requested Dr. Ralph Swan to serve as Acting Superintendent of Public Instruction. Swan had been a deputy superintendent in the department since 1953, and previously had been a teacher, principal, and county superintendent. He was an established leader in the area of in-service programs, school district reorganization, and school construction.

Dr. Swan directed the department successfully for 16 months. During this time, Dr. Swan adopted and initiated many of Governor Leader's programs. One of the more sensitive areas of state action in education involved constitutional issues of religion and ethnic integrity within the cultural-pluralistic matrix.

THE AMISH

George Leader was a farmer of Pennsylvania Dutch ancestry and proud of both aspects of his background. This pride was reflected in his respect for the "plain people," especially the Amish. Their hard-working disposition and their moral integrity strongly appealed to him. Add to this his attachment to the one-room schoolhouse, one of which he attended in his youth, and the germ of the formula for what became known as the "Pennsylvania Plan" is revealed.

During his campaign, George Leader had promised the Amish that as governor he would do all in his power to stop the jailing of the Amish who violated the compulsory school attendance laws. Since the early 1900's the Amish had been prosecuted for their resistance to the law requiring their children to attend high school. The Amish did not oppose all education. In fact, their children did attend elementary school. What they resisted for religious reasons was *high school* attendance. They considered it unnecessary and dangerous to their children's faith. Because of their strong beliefs and relentless resistance to the law, the Amish often came into conflict with local school authorities for refusing to allow their children to attend school beyond the eighth grade.

The issue had not sprung up overnight. The compulsory attendance law in Pennsylvania had been enacted in 1895— but it did not immediately send all children to school. If all the children of school age had been immediately required to attend school there would not have been enough classroom space to accommodate them. This situation persisted for many years. Enforcement of the compulsory attendance law gradually became stricter, but there were loopholes. For instance, children who lived more than two miles from school could be exempted. Exemptions could be given at age 13 to children who obtained a working permit for farm or domestic labor or other "urgent reasons." The law became more restrictive when the courts found that "urgent reason" did not mean work on the family farm.

Even more significantly the two mile exemption was ceasing to protect the Amish. The law had been modified to exempt children who lived two miles from free public transportation. The general scattering of elementary school buildings meant that Amish children usually lived within the two mile limit. In the 1950's with school district consolidation and road building, there came a push to build secondary schools in rural areas. School transportation was extended to reach children in the most rural areas. Thus, the loopholes for legal exemption from secondary school attendance that had protected the Amish from direct confrontation with school authorities were shrinking.

The Amish considered secondary education to be both worldly and unnecessary. There was another social factor which increased their resistance to secondary school attendance: their children were usually forced to leave the local community to attend the new comprehensive high schools which were being built. Interaction with non-Amish children was seen as a threat to their children's faith. The Amish communities were a total way of life. It is a sociological truism that sub-cultures maintain their distinctive manners and mores most successfully when they maintain limited communication and interaction with other groups. The Amish knew this, though not necessarily in such academic terms, and dreaded the consequences of forced association of their youth with the alien social influence of non-Amish communities.

All of these factors, the increased number of secondary schools outside the local community, the improved transportation, the stricter enforcement of compulsory attendance laws, the cultural gap between the larger society and the Amish, had resulted in a conflict which surfaced in attempts to force the Amish into conformity with the school code, and by extension, into conformity with the rest of society.

The dilemma was complex. Support for the cultural integrity of a minority group is easy to muster; at the same time, the historic association of free compulsory public education as a necessity for democratic government has persisted since Thomas Jefferson. Governor Leader knew and appreciated the Amish cultural heritage; he did not envision any threat to the larger society in making special accommodations for them. He was not naive enough to advocate a statewide return to the one-room classroom, but he believed that it could still play a role in Pennsylvania's educational system. Therefore, he directed Dr. Swan to end the coercion of the Amish.

Dr. Swan met with the Amish leaders to discuss their beliefs and needs. He designed an arrangement which satisfied both the letter of the law and the religious convictions of the Amish.

In lieu of attending public secondary schools, the Amish were permitted to establish private secondary schools.* Once a week, on Saturday, the children attended these schools and were taught by unlicensed Amish teachers. The rest of the week was spent working in their homes and on the farms, learning what the Amish needed to know to continue their religious society.

Dr. Swan, as a professional educator, had reservations about the arrangement, since the plan was not closely supervised and often the children did not attend school as the plan prescribed. The Leader initiative, however, proved to be a model for other states; a similar compromise received legal sanction in 1972 when the United States Supreme Court decided in favor of the Amish in the Yoder v. Wisconsin case.** This decision exempted Amish from compulsory school attendance on religious grounds.

George Leader's sensitivity to diversity in the midst of American cultural pluralism is best demonstrated here. His concession to the Amish Faith was a recognition of their integrity; it was not a callous disregard of the educational interests of the public at large. Leader had such confidence in the resilience of democracy that he believed protecting diversity would only make it stronger.

---

*Of course, private schools were an established constitutional alternative. The unusual accommodation which excited controversy was the very limited time and curriculum allotted to formal schooling, and the very generous acceptance of work as a home-based learning experience.

**Testimony during the case asserted that the Amish children received a more relevant education for their roles in life, possibly a better education than some of the children who attend the public secondary schools.

SPECIAL EDUCATION

Early in his Administration, Governor Leader, his brother Henry (his legislative secretary), and Dr. Swan discussed the education available to handicapped children in Pennsylvania. The Governor was aware of the inadequate educational opportunities for handicapped children, partly through his background in education, through his personal experience having a son with a visual handicap, and through first hand observation when campaigning throughout the state. He knew that the handicapped were rarely taught in the public schools and that the private residential schools provided a restricted environment. When progressive school districts held classes for the handicapped, these classes were often conducted in grim settings—in the basements, attics, or next to the restrooms, with little or no equipment. Far from being singled out for special attention, they were largely being segregated for special neglect.

Dr. Swan and Henry Leader informed the Governor that though legislation for special education existed, it was *permissive* legislation. This meant that school districts could provide special education, but were not obligated to do so. Two years before, the county school boards, had also been given the option to provide special education classes. The Governor wanted a bill which would force the school districts to provide special education for the handicapped, so that if the districts did not comply, the state could then provide the necessary services and charge the costs to the districts. Henry assured the Governor that such legislation could indeed be drafted.

Such legislation was sponsored by Representatives Susie Monroe and Louis Sherman, both of Philadelphia, and Senator Jeanette Reibman of Northampton County. The bill was introduced into the House at the end of June 1955 and passed by unanimous vote at the end of August. However, the bill did not proceed as quickly in the Senate. At this time, Governor Leader and the legislators were involved in what became a seventeen-month tax battle. As a result, the special education legislation did not pass the Senate until March of 1956. The Governor promptly signed the bill and commended, "I salute the legislature for this action, my heart brimming with gratitude and pride." The legislation realized a major objective of the Leader administration.

Positive results of the law were soon evident. When Governor Leader took office, approximately 50,000 children received some form of special education, about one-fourth of the total number requiring it. When he left office, approximately 150,000 children were enrolled in special education classes. However, Leader did not achieve all he had hoped to do for the handicapped children in Pennsylvania. He had proposed facilities at the state colleges for training special education teachers, special education for the socially and emotionally disturbed and for the gifted. These programs did, however, become reality under subsequent administrations. There is no doubt that the legislation written during Leader's term of office was the impetus for these later programs.

In February 1958, Governor Leader established the Governor's Committee on Handicapped Children, and selected Mrs. Pearl Buck Walsh* to chair it. Although the committee was not part of the Department of Public Instruction, the two bodies worked together closely. Pearl Buck was a member of the State Council of Education; she selected Gwen Zarfoss, the Department's Bureau of Special Pupil Services, as executive director. Pearl Buck had been impressed by Mrs. Zarfoss's truthful reporting of the slow progress made in some areas toward full implementation of the mandatory special education act. The Committee was charged to explore new programs to aid Pennsylvania's handicapped citizens. This committee was also directed to coordinate state government activities which related to the handicapped. The committee encouraged local communities to establish mayor's committees for handicapped citizens which would provide services for the handicapped citizens in their communities. A few areas did establish such committees and some did provide exemplary programs for the handicapped.

---

*Pearl S. Buck, the Nobel Prize-winning novelist.

THE SEARCH FOR A SUPERINTENDENT OF PUBLIC INSTRUCTION

One of the two cabinet level positions George Leader did not fill by the beginning of his term was that of Superintendent of Public Instruction. This was not from a lack of candidates or recommendations; rather, Governor Leader had not found a person who matched the criteria he had established for the position. Leader wanted radical reforms and was convinced that someone outside the department would be best able to achieve his objectives. The young governor's strong sentiments about education dictated his stubborn conviction that he must find someone who would shape up the department and provide effective leadership for Pennsylvania education.

Governor Leader approached many prominent educators inside and outside of the state, but they were either content with their current work or unwilling to accept the risks of the position. Its reputation as a political and patronage-haunted directorship was an impediment to first-class professional recruitment. The search would conclude with the identification of a person who met Leader's standards, and would also trust the Governor's assurances that he wanted both a new image and a new performance for the Department.

Thirteen months passed without success despite intense efforts by the Governor to find the right person. Leader was discouraged. The inability to find someone who would personify this new image was distressing. The Governor approached Dr. Millard Gladfelter, provost of Temple University, for advice. The Governor explained his efforts and the type of person he was searching for. Dr. Gladfelter suggested that he look among the county superintendents. The Governor then asked Dr. Gladfelter if he had anyone specially in mind. Gladfelter suggested Charles H. Boehm, Superintendent of Bucks County, whom he described as both a thinker and a doer. This to George Leader summed up the job description, for Leader admired practical theorists; "dreamers with shovels," as David Lilienthal called them.

Bucks County had recently experienced a dramatic increase in population. Faced with such a challenge, Boehm had used every opportunity to provide an excellent education program at the county level. Under his direction, Bucks County was one of the first counties to establish special education at the county level and successfully completed some school district consolidation. Governor Leader met with Dr. Boehm and decided that his many forward-looking ideas and his record of accomplishments met the criteria established for the position. Even though their similar perspectives on educational issues surely eased their working association, Leader neither wanted nor received his views rubber-stamped.

Charles H. Boehm had received his education at Keystone Normal School, and Franklin and Marshall College. He received his master's degree from Teachers College of Columbia University and his doctorate from Rutgers University. Leader's desire to minimize political influence is evidenced by the fact that Boehm was a Republican. Boehm's good faith was punctuated by his willingness to do important work at a reduced salary.

Dr. Boehm quickly reorganized the department to eliminate the prior emphasis on regulatory functions (the disbursement of money, the issuance of licenses, certificates, awards, and diplomas). His new priorities placed emphasis on curriculum development, administrative leadership, and improving school facilities. For example, the division of Child Accounting and Research was divided into two units—one for regulation and one for research. Some observers of the administration criticized the Superintendent for being too idealistic and for attempting to implement new ideas faster than the process of change would allow. All agreed on one thing, Boehm shook up the Department of Public Instruction. This was what the Governor had intended. In fact, Leader later asserted that Boehm was the best thing that ever happened to the Department of Public Instruction.

A key problem of reorganization was attracting qualified people to fill the vacant posts in the department. Superintendent Boehm was competing with private industry that offered higher salaries and job security. But, improved salaries and the positive non-political recruitment campaign drew qualified candidates for professional positions in the department; when Dr. Boehm found none, he used consultants. Through his recruiting efforts, Dr. Boehm was able to raise the number of persons holding doctorates from four in 1956, to thirty in 1964, when his term ended after Governor Scranton's election.

Part of Superintendent Boehm's recruitment program was the placement of women and minorities in professional positions in the department. In this he was somewhat less successful than he was in increasing the number of doctorates, however, he was able to recruit some professionals from minority groups. One such person was Dr. Catherine Coleman, who was later promoted to Director of the Bureau of Teacher Education. She was the first black person and the second woman to direct a bureau in the Department of Public Instruction.

Dr. Boehm recalled that recruiting was very difficult because of the dubious professional reputation which the Department of Public Instruction had earned. One superintendent at a national convention described the Superintendency of Public Instruction in Pennsylvania as the most difficult in the country because of the political nature of the state. Pennsylvania's reputation for low pay and poor job security was well known and hindered Superintendent Boehm's search for talented educators. However, there was an influx of qualified people, and they were often directly sponsored by the governor's office when other political sponsorship was not forth coming.

In 1955, Pennsylvania retained only two-thirds of the graduates of its teachers colleges, for higher salaries in neighboring states attracted many teachers needed in this state. Governor Leader advocated higher salaries to attract better teachers, thereby improving the quality of Pennsylvania's education. In mid-1956, he signed House Bill 583, which moved the state's teacher salaries from one of the lowest to fifteenth in the nation. Minimum and maximum salaries were raised, and the average salary increased to $5,000 in 1959.

CURRICULUM

Superintendent Boehm's emphasis on curriculum development as an important aspect of the leadership role of the new Department of Public Instruction was reflected in the departmental reorganization. Of the existing seven bureaus, only one was even partially concerned with curriculum. After Boehm's reorganization, three of 12 departments were specifically devoted to curriculum.

In the 1950's educators stressed the importance of a strong curriculum for quality education. Evidencing this concern, a State Curriculum Commission was formed to evaluate the state curriculum and recommend improvements. Three aspects of the basic curriculum received primary attention: English, mathematics and science, and social studies. The main focus was on high schools where basic requirements were found to be unreasonably low.

Dr. Boehm was interested in total involvement in reform of Pennsylvania's curriculum, from kindergarten to teacher training. Curriculum was on the agenda for most of the commissions studying the educational system of Pennsylvania. Total involvement, though, culminated in the Governor's Conference on the Improvement of Instruction. Governor Leader announced the plan for the conference in December 1957. One hundred educators and laymen were to be invited to reappraise the entire instructional program of Pennsylvania schools, kindergarten through twelfth grade. One of the delegates' main concerns was to be the school system's minimum requirements which had not changed for twenty years.

The reaction to the conference was surprising. The members of the various commissions on education were invited but surprisingly many individuals and organizations expressed interest and demanded representation. Before long, the invitation list exceeded 300 names including educators, legislators, clergymen, and laypersons. The intense interest in the conference came mainly from confusion about its purpose. Somehow people got the idea that the conference had been called to prepare a plan for extending the school year or lengthening the school week to six days. The more news coverage the conference received, the more excitement it generated and it soon obtained the status of a major public event.

The conference actually was convened to explore problems relating to mathematics, science, English, social studies, adult education, and pupil guidance. One basic question asked about each of the general areas of curriculum was whether school children in Pennsylvania were receiving sufficient instruction in each subject. Some questions posed to the conference delegates were sensitive such as "should social studies teachers be free to discuss controversial topics?" This question related to the study of communism. Both George Leader and Charles Boehm felt that no one could understand an unknown, and if communism was an unknown, then children could not evaluate it. This position was unpopular in the shadow of the McCarthy era, but Boehm added a study of communism to the public school curriculum. The results were gratifying. The American Legion awarded this program its endorsement as unimpeachably American.

While the conference produced a number of recommendations for the improvement of instruction in Pennsylvania, it did not establish a six day school week. As a result of the conference, the requirements for high school graduation were increased.

Pennsylvania's educational reforms were well underway before the Russians launched the first Sputnik satellite, a fact which Governor Leader often stressed proudly in his speeches. The Russian's scientific advances shook the American people; the attention of politicians and educators turned to mathematics and science. Sputnik was the catalyst which the Governor needed to push his educational reforms. Only at the end of his administration did the Federal government produce the needed legislation which would assist the states in accelerating their mathematic and science programs at all levels. This came in the form of the National Defense Education Act, passed in the summer of 1958. Because of the advances made in its school curriculum and the studies made on the needs of the educational system in the state, Pennsylvania's Department of Public Instruction was one of the first to submit plans for the use of NDEA funds.

SCHOOL CONSTRUCTION

One of the most apparent and urgent needs of the Pennsylvania school system was for safe, comfortable, and adequate school buildings. The depression and the Second World

War had curtailed new school construction. Certain limited measures had been taken during the Fine administration to alleviate the problem. For example, the ceiling for school construction loans had been raised to $425 million. The Leader administration now put together a bill which raised the ceiling by another $500 million. The Governor called this support the "most extensive program of its kind ever undertaken by any government agency." When the Governor signed the bill in March 1956, it raised the school construction ceiling to $925 million to be used through 1959. This legislation funded 659 schools accommodating more than 300,000 children. This school building program became increasingly significant in the last year of his administration, when a recession occurred, and the administration staff accelerated public works projects to reduce the effects of unemployment caused by the recession.

SCHOOL DISTRICT REORGANIZATION

Although school district consolidation did not begin during the Leader administration, significant advances were made in those four years. Pennsylvania school district consolidation must be seen against the backdrop of the times. Local control had been supreme, to the extent that in 1935 there were 2,854 school districts in the State, a few of which did not employ a single teacher or operate a school. These districts sent their children to adjoining districts and paid their tuition.

During the 1950's the shortage of adequate schools for the rapidly growing school age population became acute. An earlier law granted a yearly two hundred dollar bonus to any school district for each one-room school closed. This encouraged the elimination of the one-room schoolhouses but increased the shortage of adequate school buildings. The need for secondary schools was especially grave and the projected enrollments made it imperative to provide more buildings. The need for new secondary schools aided the move toward large school districts.

When Leader took office, earlier consolidation efforts had reduced the number of school districts to 2,436. Many of these were too small to make secondary school construction feasible. Instead, they depended on tuition arrangements with adjacent districts for high schools for their students. So towns with small secondary schools, barely adequate for their own needs, would often find themselves educating the children of surrounding townships. This situation not only decreased educational quality, but also resulted in over-crowded facilities. Despite the progress, a note of pessimism came through in Boehm's final report to the Governor. Although the number of districts had been reduced by 87 to 2,351, it would take fifty years at that rate to reduce Pennsylvania school districts to a workable number. Some thought was given to the possibility of establishing intermediate units, but they remained only possibilities until the 1970's.

HIGHER EDUCATION

Governor Leader was particularly interested in higher education. He often spoke of his higher education program as a conservation effort, "While we are busy conserving our natural resources, we must never forget that our children are our greatest resources and there should be adequate opportunity for them in Pennsylvania's institutions of higher education." Pennsylvania had numerous colleges and universities, and yet only half of the high school graduates applying for colleges could find places in Pennsylvania colleges.

Because of the growing population, it was important that the problem of inadequate opportunities for higher education be tackled immediately. The Leader administration launched a two-front attack: one on the 14 state-owned teachers colleges, and the other on higher education in general. The Governor was able to affect more changes in the state-owned institutions than in the other areas of higher education. However, Leader's plan for higher education was substantially implemented in later administrations.

The enrollment at each of the state-owned teacher colleges was under 1,000 students. Because of Pennsylvania's shortage of teachers, the Governor wanted to expand these colleges but several were already landlocked by their surrounding communities. The Governor discovered that only one college had a long-range plan. So the first necessity, in the expansion of the state colleges, was to prepare campus plans for all of the state teacher colleges. After plans were prepared, Governor Leader requested funds from the legislature for physical plant expansion. As a result, construction was completed, begun, or placed under design at all 14 state colleges by the end of the Leader administration. Eleven schools began dormitories to house 2,800 students. In addition, one million dollars was allocated to these schools for the purchase of land.

Changes in basic curricular design prepared the state teacher colleges for the transition to state colleges. Approximately 80 percent of the courses had been either educational methods or other educational classes. In response to the reforms in the public school system, the curriculum at these institutions was changed to 50 percent education and 50 percent liberal art courses; this gave the teachers a stronger base in the substantive areas. This shift in emphasis meant a shift in the nature of the faculty. The change from teacher colleges to state colleges, which occurred in 1960, was facilitated by Leader's efforts because the education faculties had already been reduced and the liberal arts faculties expanded. This change in faculty and planned campus expansion assisted Pennsylvania to meet the growing demand for higher education in the 1960's and 1970's. Rather than building new institutions, Pennsylvania was able to expand its 14 state colleges to accommodate many students in broad programs of learning.

The respect that Governor Leader had for higher education was evident not only in what he said about it, but also in the people he chose to assist him. His advisory committee was composed of academics; some of his department heads and staff of the Office of Administration were faculty members of Pennsylvania colleges. In 1956, Leader established the Commission on Higher Education to prepare a report outlining the needs of higher education in Pennsylvania for the next twenty years. This Commission was chaired by Dr. Paul Anderson, President of Chatham College, and included representatives from large, small, private, and public institutions. The Governor gave this group the freedom to investigate any aspect of higher education. The Commission reported directly to the Governor, rather than to the Department of Public Instruction.

The Commission took a full year to complete its report, but submitted it too late for the Governor to have legislation prepared for the 1956 session. The report identified three basic programs later translated into legislation: scholarships, student aid loans, and community colleges. These programs were to be supported by a 1¢ tax on softdrinks. However, the Republicans controlled both houses of the legislature in 1957, and they were not as sympathetic as the Democrats to the Governor's programs. The media and educators throughout the state praised Leader's proposal, however, the lawmakers called it "idealistic, socialistic, and pie-in-the-sky." The Governor argued quite strongly for passage of his higher education program, his case strengthened by the launching of Sputnik. In one speech he stated:

> We must realize that a crash program of higher education is just as immediate a need as a crash program for guided missiles. Obviously, America must meet this challenge in the classroom and meet it quickly. For not only must we catch up but we must stay ahead of a fleet and tireless opponent. We must first meet the need for higher education, if we are to win the race for survival.

When Governor Leader met resistance to his proposed legislation for higher education, he vowed to "fight and keep on fighting" for legislation he considered absolutely necessary for the state and the nation. He promised to place the facts before the people in an attempt to pressure the reluctant legislators to enact the legislation. Leader had used the same tactic during the tax battle and much to his disappointment his popular campaign for higher education reform met the same fate as his classified income tax—defeat. Even inviting supporters of his higher education bill to Harrisburg, a gesture which helped establish the Fair Employment Practice Council, was of no avail in this battle. Pennsylvania may have been ready for student aid and community colleges, but Pennsylvania politicians were not.

THE DEPARTMENT OF WELFARE

The most dramatic changes effected during the Leader administration came in the Department of Welfare. There were many political jobs available in this department, especially in the state mental institutions. These positions were traditionally bestowed by the Governor as favors and rewards to county chairmen and other political leaders. The mental institutions suffered because of patronage, which perpetrated an attitude in state workers that Governor Leader in a speech, excoriated as "one of clock-punching indifference to the important work being done to help our mentally ill. It is one of inflexible bureaucracy, of built-in defeatism, of yawning routine, of tangled red tape." The Department of Welfare had more than its share of indifferent employees. It was not surprising that the basic function of the state mental health program was custodial care rather than treatment.

It is arguable that the Department of Welfare prior to Leader's administration had not deserved its name. It was not professionalized. Only a small minority of its staff, including supervisory personnel had any social work education, let alone degrees or certification as professional social workers. The process of "professionalizing" the Commonwealth's welfare services began during Leader's administration. This would be reflected in new attention to survey and research; effective supervision, operation and control of institutional conditions; the identification of problem areas and alternatives; and the professionalizing of staff by hiring professionals and initiating on-the-job training.

Governor Leader's philosophy of government was based on one of Abraham Lincoln's ideas that government exists to provide for those citizens unable to provide for themselves. One of the major objectives of the Leader administration was to correct the deplorable condition of the state mental institutions. Many of these conditions had been outlined in the pre-inaugural report. They were not less horrible because they were common to most states, because the care of the mentally ill was a national disgrace. Leader proposed reforms where he could—in Pennsylvania.

The pre-inaugural study made 42 recommendations for improving the Department of Welfare and its services. The authors of the report urged the department to remove the administrative responsibilities of the state mental hospitals from their boards of trustees, to hire professionals, to provide adequate treatment, and to reduce the overcrowding in the institutions. With respect to children's services, the authors called for a complete revamping of the department's role. It pointed out that private agencies and other branches of state government were critical of the Department of Welfare's activities, especially in the area of juvenile delinquents and "mental defectives."

SELECTION OF THE SECRETARY OF WELFARE

George Leader did not have much difficulty finding his Secretary of Welfare. Harry Shapiro, a Philadelphia lawyer and ex-state senator, stood out as an individual who was committed to providing a better way of life for the needy of the State. Senator Shapiro was credited with the writing of the State's Mental Health Act in the 1930's, legislation which was still in effect.

Shapiro had the unique distinction of having served as the leader of both parties in the Senate. The story is told that Senator Shapiro, initially a Republican, had basic disagreements with his party; one day he simply stood up in the Senate chamber and walked over to the Democratic side. He was subsequently elected for two more senate terms as a Democrat. Although Shapiro was a politician, he was not selected by Governor Leader because of his political connections. Rather Leader selected Harry Shapiro because of his qualifications and interest in the field of welfare. Senator Shapiro had been chairman of a State Senate Committee to investigate conditions at Philadelphia State Hospital and served as a trustee of Mount Sinai Hospital.

Secretary Shapiro was a dedicated but stubborn man, who was especially impatient with red tape. This trait often brought him into conflict with other governmental units, such as when he established a college training program for employees without legislative approval and purchased television sets for the mental hospitals without proper authorization, yet his drive and motivation produced results and were a source of motivation to those around him. But his persistance was often a source of irritation to many, especially the staff of the Office of Administration who accused him of ignoring regulations and exceeding his budget. Many people in state government, especially the legislators, felt that he wanted too much too fast.

Governor Leader was often criticized for Shapiro's actions by local politicians who saw their control of patronage positions diminish. Prior to the Leader administration, only about 300 of the 14,000 positions in the Department of Welfare were not under the patronage system. The Governor defended the Secretary from political attacks and criticism leveled against what was sometimes referred to as the welfare's "fat budget." Leader considered Shapiro the only person in Pennsylvania capable of correcting in a matter of months, a situation that had taken 20 years of neglect to create. The Governor and the Secretary agreed on most welfare issues, and the Secretary welcomed Leader's support.

INVESTIGATIONS

Secretary Shapiro did not sit in his office in Harrisburg and establish policies based solely on statistics. He personally visited the institutions to see for himself how the mental patients and juveniles were treated. Early in the administration, he visited the Laurelton State Village and, as the result of the conditions he found in one cottage, ordered the cottage closed. This, of course, antagonized the institution's board of trustees which were responsible for the activities and conditions of the institution. Secretary Shapiro reported that he had taken his findings to the board, but since they seemed unwilling or unable to improve the situation, he had ordered the cottage closed. The Secretary sent two independent investigators to confirm his findings. They reported that the girls in the Johnston Cottage were exposed to many abuses, such as the practice of isolation as a means of punishment. The record books had been removed from the cottage and when they were returned, they revealed that administrators

54

often gave verbal directions to the matrons of the cottage as to how to deal with troublemakers. Girls were placed in isolation for up to four weeks when they were nasty to the matrons, the water in the toilets in the rooms would be shut off for two or three days, leaving the girls in a growing stench. One of the dieticians was found to be syphilitic and there were reports of homosexuality in another cottage. Shapiro ordered these practices stopped and the clean-up and shake-up of the state welfare institutions began. As a result of this investigation and visits by the Secretary at other institutions many instances of patient abuses and inadequate care were exposed and eliminated. Conditions reminiscent of the Dark Ages were remedied, and Pennsylvania's mental health program entered the twentieth century.

The Secretary also required some hospital employees living on hospital property to leave and find their own housing. The Secretary could not tolerate this situation in light of the overcrowded conditions at state facilities. Shapiro should not be thought to have been authoritarian, despite his penchant for directness; he knew his responsibilities, took them seriously, and dared to act.

CHANGE IN PHILOSOPHY

For centuries, the mentally ill were treated as witches, devils, or fools. At worst, they were eliminated and at best, they were placed in institutions and provided with minimal food and shelter. The general population feared the mentally ill and institutionalization was considered the most humane way of "dealing" with them. Pennsylvania was not eliminating its mentally ill in a primitive way, but certainly the State was not dealing with the patients in any way which could have been considered modern. Two factors blocked proper treatment of the mentally ill: the politics of economy and neglect, and the popular belief that mental disease was something horrible and evil.

Politics reduced the status of mental patients to that of prisoners. The politically controlled boards of trustees of the state mental institutions used favoritism as the criteria for hiring hospital personnel. Low salaries, due to inadequate appropriations, added to the difficulty of obtaining capable personnel. The insufficient appropriations can be partly explained by the unpopularity of welfare programs. They were not vote-getters like road construction. Patronage also meant no job security, so, qualified persons were difficult to attract. They preferred work in other state and private agencies. Even with committed and qualified people, the system was structured to discourage innovation. Politicians were staunch supporters of the status quo. A great idea could easily be rendered ineffective by a lack of funds or by resistance from a supervisor or other employees.

This situation required a two-pronged attack, each facet depended on the other for success. An influx of qualified professionals would accomplish little without a fundamental change in department philosophy. Equally, a change of philosophy without talented personnel would have little or no effect. Secretary Shapiro achieved both objectives: the change in philosophy and the recruitment of new employees.

Pennsylvania's welfare system included twenty-three institutions for the mentally ill and mentally retarded, which housed a population of 47,000. Ten state general hospitals and one training school for juvenile delinquents were under the jurisdiction of the Department of Welfare. The mental institutions were operated under the philosophy of custodial care. This meant that the State was the receptacle for all the unwanted individuals in the State and that these individuals were considered to be of no benefit to society. They were only liabilities that took from the General Fund and contributed nothing. Pennsylvania tax payers were willing to pay for custodial care, because they knew of no alternative and because it was an inexpensive way of ridding their communities of misfits. Once these people were institutionalized, most people were not concerned about their welfare. If they were treated as they had been treated for centuries, that was all that was to be expected of the system.

Here the patronage system and traditional concepts of mental illness and custodial care supported one another. Custodial care seemed to be the easiest and cheapest way to deal with social outcasts. The patronage system excelled at providing personnel at levels other than those of the technical and professional nature, the type which would have been needed to provide treatment rather than custody. Politicans could easily justify this system because few people were clamoring for change.

The Department of Welfare underwent a change in philosophy during Leader's administration. Secretary Shapiro explained this change when he told the institution superintendents that "we propose to maintain the human dignity of the individual patient by treating the problem irrespective of outmoded and confusing legal and social labels, and to restore and maintain the dignity and self-respect of all personnel in the institutions." This goal was to be achieved through treatment rather than custodial care which, Shapiro emphasized, had often led to neglect and cruelty.

TOURS BY THE GOVERNOR

After about a year in office, Leader announced that he would personally visit several state mental institutions to see firsthand what progress had been made and what problems still remained. He asserted that statistics and budget figures alone did not adequately describe what remained to be accomplished. The Governor invited legislators, clergymen, labor leaders, persons from private welfare agencies, and the press to accompany himself and Secretary Shapiro on the tours. He began with a tour of Mayview State Hospital, located near Pittsburgh. The Governor asked the press not to dramatize the visits but rather to report the existing problems and the accomplishments of the Department of Welfare in the mental health area.

The Governor's personal secretary, Mary Ressler, recalled that the Governor was particularly moved by these visits; their impact was reflected in his mood the day following the tours. His personal commitment to improve welfare services for these neglected citizens was intensified as a result of his trips.

The Governor recalled that, after walking through the institutions he developed pains in the calves of his legs caused by the slippery floors. These floors had been the cause of numerous broken hips in the mental institutions and the

Governor now understood why. The maintenance people used regular wax, polished to the smoothest shine. When Leader asked them why they did not use non-skid wax, the maintenance people responded that they could not obtain it. The Governor instructed them to use a non-skid wax which he remembered from his Navy days. After he received a report indicating their inability to locate the non-skid wax, Leader contacted the Navy to obtain the specifications for the non-skid wax. As a result of using this Navy-type non-skid wax, the old and infirmed did not have to navigate the dangerously slick corridors.

Slick floors were a minor problem compared to the deplorable conditions in the state mental institutions. In December of 1955, Governor Leader addressed the General Assembly to highlight the need for improvements in these facilities. The Governor reported instances of collapsing auditoriums, corroded beams, and buckled kitchen floors. Some sections or wings of institutions were abandoned, because there were no funds for repairs. Only 50¢ a day was budgeted for food per patient ($15.00 per month), and in one case, unpastuerized milk was used. In another institution, orange juice was so scarce that only those children in critical need received any at all. The lack of privacy probably had the greatest affect on the Governor. The overcrowding and the common practice of allowing patients to remain partially dressed were dehumanizing. The Governor regarded lines of toilets without partitions as one of the worst examples of the lack of privacy in the state institutions. Overcrowding was blatant. There were cots in corridors, alcoves, dayrooms, and the wards were filled to more than double their expected capacity.

But physical conditions were not the only things which were evident as problems in the institutions. The inadequate number of personnel was readily apparent. Although the recommended norm ratio was one physician for every 95 patients, in one institution there was only one physician for 290 patients, and in another, there was only one psychiatrist for 1,400 patients.*

---

*Simple arithmetic shows that in a 250 day year (of eight hour days), each patient would have less than 1½ hours of psychiatric time annually.

The Governor pleaded with the legislature not to make the comfortable more comfortable, but only for justice. Human decency was at stake here, not luxury. In his address to the General Assembly, George Leader emphasized that, unlike labor, business, or industry, the mentally ill and retarded did not have strong lobbyists to represent them in the halls of the capital. They were not a bloc of voters to whom politicians had to cater. The elected officials of the State were responsible for these people, and the Governor urged the legislators to live up to their responsibility.

The legislature responded to the criticism of being a do-nothing legislature and to the pleas of the Governor and Secretary Shapiro by approving legislation which reorganized the Bureau of Mental Health and by providing appropriations for increased staff, new construction, and renovation of existing facilities.

PERSONNEL

The custodial care or "warehousing" of patients could have continued, even if the gross overcrowding and poor facilities were eliminated. Little would have changed except the superficial appearance of the institutions. As long as the institutions remained primarily a place to dump people until they died, rather than a place where they were sent to be helped and even cured, these institutions would remain custodial in nature. That there were mental hospitals without psychiatrists and a terrible inadequacy of medical doctors, nurses, therapists, and other personnel was unjustifiable by any standard of decency. Many mental patients spent their entire time in these institutions without once seeing a psychiatrist.

The state welfare institutions were ready for a change and theories of prevention and treatment were growing nationwide. A better way was known and qualified people could be pressed into service to bring about the change. The change from custodial care to prevention and cure required modern facilities, qualified personnel, and a progressive perspective on mental illness. As Secretary Shapiro stated in his final report to the Governor, "this change represents the difference between existing and living; between cure and custody; between the helping hand and the cold shoulder."

Norman Lourie had written part of the welfare pre-inauguration report and briefed Secretary Shapiro about the department's needs. Lourie had been the executive director of the Association for Jewish Children of Philadelphia and was a child welfare consultant for the Fels Institute, at the University of Pennsylvania. The report identified a need for an executive deputy. Secretary Shapiro agreed with this recommendation and chose Norman Lourie for the position. Deputy Lourie's main duty was the recruitment of personnel. Since he had scrutinized the department closely in the pre-inauguration report, he knew that there were some qualified persons in the department. However, as in many other departments, many of the unqualified persons found employment elsewhere, anticipating removal by the new party. Others were forced to retire because of superannuation. And finally, some persons were removed because of incompetence. So the large task was not so much removing personnel, but rather finding qualified persons to replace and increase the staffs at the mental institutions.

The largest push for qualified personnel came with "Operation Opportunity" in September of 1956. The goal of this recruitment program was to hire 2,300 persons in the field of mental health. This included 189 psychiatrists and medical doctors, 82 clinical psychologists, 450 psychiatric nurses, 1,000 psychiatric aids, 319 occupational therapists and patient activity people; 200 social workers, and 60 special education teachers. In order to accomplish that goal, the salary scales had to be upgraded to make them competitive with other states and private agencies. The salary improvements were accomplished with an appropriation from the legislature.

It was, of course, essential to remove these positions from the patronage system. This was accomplished by executive civil service orders from the executive board.* These professional positions were removed from the patronage

---

*For more details about the executive board, see Civil Service, page 178.

system thus insuring better job security. Governor Leader had wanted the Legislators to place technical and professional positions under civil service, but they refused. However, the executive civil service protection was not much more secure than the patronage system because a new governor could remove it. But, non-partisan hiring and limited job security was preferable to the political practices which had been dominant for so long in Pennsylvania's state hospitals.

"Operation Opportunity" included a mass media campaign to announce changes in the Department of Welfare to the public and to professionals in the mental health field. Professionals were encouraged to investigate the possibility of working for the state. The Governor himself did the first series of radio spots for the recruitment program. The search for and recruitment of mental health professionals was not limited to Pennsylvania. National organizations and journals were used to advertise Pennsylvania's recruitment drive.

CHANGES

The first piece of legislation authorized the reorganization of the Bureau of Mental Health and gave the department more control over mental health programs throughout the state. The Mental Health Advisory Council had conducted a national search and recommended Dr. Robert Matthews to the Governor. Matthews was appointed as the Commissioner of Mental Health in charge of the Bureau. The Commissioner was hired at a salary equal to that of the Governor's. The Council, composed of eighteen mental health professionals or persons active in that area, advised the Secretary and the Governor on mental health policy and programs.

One of the most significant aspects of the reorganization was the change in status of the boards of trustees of the state mental institutions. They were divested of administrative responsibilities for the institutions and became simply advisory bodies for the institutions' superintendents. Control of the institutions was in effect transferred to the Department of Welfare, thus largely removing partisan policies from the operation of the state mental institutions.

Other legislation provided resources to initiate a community mental health program in the Philadelphia area. This program coordinated the efforts of medical schools, welfare agencies, the state and city Bureaus of Mental Health, and the state institutions in an effort to prevent and treat mental illness. Throughout the State, the department began a campaign to establish mental health programs at the community level for prevention and rehabilitation.

Research was a key element in the new approach to combatting and curing mental illness. The administration sought and obtained legislative approval to form the Mental Health Research Foundation. This panel of ten persons, chaired by the Secretary of Welfare, was responsible for coordinating, promoting, and evaluating proposed mental health research projects in the State. The Foundation was authorized to receive and disburse both public and private money for mental health research. In conjunction with this Foundation, the Eastern Pennsylvania Psychiatric Institute opened a research and training facility for Pennsylvania's mental health system.

A $26,500,000 appropriation was used to raise the salaries of state hospital employees and to hire approximately 1,300 new professionals, many through "Operation Opportunity." But the most impressive accomplishment of the Leader administration in the area of mental health was the decrease in population at the state institutions while admissions remained constant. This meant that the infusion of professionals, funds for improvements, the modern leadership, and progressive programs began to pay off in the number of individuals who were returning to their families and loved ones. Former mental patients were restored to useful, productive lives rather than being hidden away in a state hospital.

This program did not go unnoticed by the citizens of Pennsylvania. Often, while the Governor was touring the state for speaking engagements or campaigning for the U.S. Senate, individuals would come up to him and thank him for returning a spouse or child to the family.

CHILD SERVICES

The second thrust of the Department of Welfare during Leader's administration was in the area of child services. The department had been severely criticized for the inadequacies of its child services program. The child services were directed at the juvenile delinquents, the emotionally disturbed, and to dependent or neglected children. The enormous problem of juvenile delinquency was evident from the number of children committed to institutions by juvenile courts in Pennsylvania. Approximately 2,500 children per year were committed, the highest number in the nation.

As in the area of mental health, Governor Leader and Secretary Shapiro stressed that prevention and treatment were better than custody. Therefore, his administration advocated legislation to improve child services. The Governor stressed often that children were not born bad and did not have to remain problems. Incarceration, he asserted, reduced their chances of becoming productive citizens.

The first objective in this area was to improve the only state-owned and operated youth training center, located at Morganza. Secretary Shapiro stated that this institution suffered from "too little program and too much politics." He ordered the dismissal of political appointees and the retirement of superannuated employees. These were replaced by younger, better trained individuals. The Secretary also mandated the elimination of all inhumane places of confinement. These changes involved a renovation of the deteriorated facilities at the school and a progressive program of treatment and training. The staff was increased to provide the medical, social, and educational care which the youths deserved.

Pennsylvania had not only the highest number of children committed by juvenile courts, but also the dubious distinction of being the only state which did not assist counties with the care of dependent, neglected, and delinquent children in institutions run by local governments. This situation was corrected by Act 406, which authorized the Department of Welfare to aid the county programs. This legislation went further and, as the Governor and Secretary Shapiro had desired, established centers for the diagnosis and evaluation of problem children.

The orientation for the new child services was toward research and treatment. Because of the increase in juvenile delinquency, there was great concern for the identification of its causes. One explanation attributed this increase to the social circumstances caused by the Second World War. The stance of the Leader administration was not to remove these misdirected and troubled children from society, but to rehabilitate them, to study the causes of their problems, and to seek effective preventative measures. The department assumed a position of leadership by developing standards of treatment and training for the twenty-one private and county juvenile institutions and for the state school at Morganza. The department, for the first time, was authorized to participate in the important process of placing delinquents in institutions. Prior to this time, the courts had assumed total authority over placement.

One new program for juveniles was the creation of camps in the state forests. Established in conjunction with the Department of Forest and Waters, it was modeled on the CCC camps of the depression era. The purpose of these camps was to remove juvenile delinquents from their environment and place them in new surroundings, where they would receive proper social, psychological, or educational treatment and training, according to their needs. These camps, like the CCC's, not only benefited the youths but also developed and maintained the state forests and parks.

Changes in state involvements with the institutions and new programs like the juvenile camps were attempts by the Department of Welfare to alter a growing pattern of repeating offenders. As in the area of mental health, early treatment was seen as the method most likely to cure. Professionals in the Leader administration believed that custodial care or incarceration of juvenile offenders prepared them for a life that would bring them back to the state institutions, either as patients or as prisoners.

Because state borders are open and unrestricted, the State encountered many problems with "jurisdiction jumpers" some of whom were juvenile delinquents. Runaways, escapees, and parole violators often left their states to avoid apprehension. The mobile state of postwar population often meant the children on parole would legitimately move with their families, making parole supervision difficult or practically impossible.

Recognition of these problems led to the development of the Interstate Compact on Juveniles during Leader's administration. This simplified the procedures for returning runaways and escapees. The exchange of children who needed specialized care not available in the child's home state was also facilitated. As well, the compact provided for the easy transfer of parole supervision between states. Pennsylvania's power to control juvenile delinquency was extended beyond the children who passed through its courts.

THE STATE GENERAL HOSPITALS

No discussion of the Department of Welfare is complete without a discussion of the state general hospitals and the department's involvement with the Hill-Burton program, a federally funded program for hospital construction.

The operation of the ten general hospitals was labelled anachronistic in the pre-inaugural reports prepared for Leader. These hospitals were established originally to provide medical and surgical facilities in mining communities, but in 1939 they were renamed "general hospitals" and serviced a broader population.

The state financed these hospitals without contributions from the local communities; therefore, ten communities enjoyed special privileges which the other communities in the State did not receive. Once established, state funding is politically difficult to withdraw.

From Leader's term onward, administrations have wanted the state to disassociate itself from the operation of the general hospitals. As yet, this has not happened, and the state hospitals are run by local boards of trustees appointed by politicians. Interest groups have blocked legislative efforts to terminate state involvement. Paradoxically, state general hospitals have remained under the control of the local boards, but the state mental hospitals were made advisory.

The Department of Welfare also supervised private hospitals and was responsible for the Hill-Burton program. The

65

pre-inaugural study suggested that the administration of the Hill-Burton program was more germane to the Department of Health and recommended that administration responsibility be transferred from the Department of Welfare. The recommendation was not implemented, and the department continued the Hill-Burton program. Two significant uses of the Hill-Burton funds during Leader's administration were the extent to which the funds supplemented the mental health program and their use in public works projects during the 1958 recession. Space for 783 additional psychiatric patients was provided in thirty-one general hospitals during Leader's term in office. Between 1948 and 1955 only seventeen new spaces had been allotted. This meant that the general hospitals provided more local care for mental health patients. Secretary Shapiro obtained approval to accelerate $20,000,000 of hospital construction which had been scheduled for 1959, to offset a high level of unemployment during the 1958 recession.

THE MERGER OF WELFARE AND PUBLIC ASSISTANCE

The Chesterman Report, a survey of the executive branch made during the Fine administration, recommended the consolidation of the Departments of Health, Welfare, and Public Assistance. The legislature, during the Fine administration, rejected the proposed merger, Governor Fine passed the recommendations for the merger to Governor Leader. Leader's staff did not favor this merger, because it would have created a department of enormous size and complicate administrative functions. But there was a feeling in the administration that the responsibilities of some departments would be better performed by other departments. As a matter of fact, some 400 administration reorganization bills remained unpassed by the legislature in the Leader administration, but the merger of Welfare and Public Assistance was achieved.

Republican legislators did not like Secretary Shapiro, partly because of his political defection and they would have liked to have had him removed. They introduced a bill to abolish the Department of Welfare and transfer its responsibilities to four other departments, thereby eliminating the position of Secretary of Welfare. Governor Leader's attention was drawn to the bill by Henry Leader, his legislative secretary, who advised the Governor that opposition to the bill would appear regressive. Henry pointed out that the Departments of Welfare and Public Assistance had been combined in the majority of states. Because the administration did not accept the bill as written, Henry informed the bill's sponsors that certain changes were necessary to obtain executive support. Having secured the consent of the sponsors to have the bill redrafted, administrative attorneys completely rewrote the bill leaving only its original number. The new bill was passed in July of 1957, but the actual merger did not occur until 1958. As with many other actions taken by the Leader administration, research and analysis, rather than political consideration were used to determine how to best effect the merger of the two departments. The legislation required the Governor to establish a committee to review the consolidation experiences of other states. In April of 1958, the committee submitted its report to the Governor. At this time and with no warning, Secretary Shapiro submitted his resignation to the Governor. Rather than accept his resignation, Leader urged Shapiro to become the first Secretary of the new Department of Public Welfare, stating that, "under your direction the Department of Welfare had done much to give a new sense of hope and dignity to troubled and sick men, women, and children. Yet as we often have agreed, this is only a good beginning. There is still much to be done." Harry Shapiro accepted the position and served out the remaining months of the administration as the Secretary of Public Welfare which now consisted of six commissions, one of which was the Commission of Public Assistance.

Governor Leader was proud of the accomplishments in welfare areas, and this pride began with his great confidence in the person in charge. These achievements included: (1) modernized and augmented support of the mental health program; (2) the extension and development of child welfare services; (3) the weakening of political domination of the state mental hospital boards of these institutions, and extensive and sucessful recruitment of professional employees.

Consistent with Leader's philosophy, the goals of the welfare program were both humane and practical. Research, study, and analysis identified issues and disciplined policy formation. When Leader and the persons he chose to trust moved into action, they kept individuals in mind and did not substitute paperwork for public concern.

DEPARTMENT OF PUBLIC ASSISTANCE

Unlike the dramatic changes which were evident in the Department of Welfare, the Department of Public Assistance, except for the merger of the two departments, remained very much as it had been under previous administrations. This continuity was probably due to the Department of Public Assistance's non-involvement in the pattern of political abuses which had afflicted the Department of Welfare.

The Department of Public Assistance was created by statute in 1937, in response to federal "New Deal" laws which provided funds for state public assistance efforts. This statute was one of several progressive, New Deal laws passed during the democratic term of Governor Earle. Ruth Grigg Horting helped draft the public assistance legislation; in 1937, she was the first woman elected from Lancaster County to the Pennsylvania House of Representatives.

Like the creation of the Bureau of Employment Security in the Department of Labor and Industry, the Department of Public Assistance was established to disburse the federal funds which were made available to the states. Federal money matched state funds in the assistance program. In areas where federal funds were involved, federal regulations required a merit system for employment; this safeguard minimized political influence within the Department of Public Assistance.

THE PRE-INAUGURAL STUDY

The pre-inaugural study done by Dr. Raymond Bowman of the University of Pennsylvania reported the quality of the personnel in the department to be quite good, apparently due to civil service requirements. The report contradicted the gloomy predictions of some politicians, who predicted that the merit system would create a pool of non-removable, incompetent employees. Dr. Bowman found that there had been a number of salutory dismissals in the department despite the civil service system, and that entrenched incompetence did not seem to be the inevitable result of the merit system. The study focused on the problem that every new Public Assistance Secretary faces: how to minimize the state's contribution to public assistance and maximize assistance to needy people. Some discretion was possible due to the nature of the public assistance law, yet most of the flexibility depended on the classification of the needy. The report made three other recommendations: 1) to have the Secretary select a deputy to handle routine matters, thus enabling the Secretary to deal with the larger problems in the department and county offices; 2) to have public assistance provide nursing home care; and 3) confront the problem of residency.

SELECTION OF THE SECRETARY

In the selection of the Secretary of Public Assistance, George Leader had to weigh several considerations. He sought a cabinet balanced with both politicians and professionals who represented most geographic regions and minority groups. Governor Fine had selected a woman for the post of Public Assistance and Leader saw this precedent as a desirable way to have women's interest represented in his cabinet. Ruth Horting was politically active, both as a legislator and as vice-chairman of the Democratic State Committee. At that time she was considered one of the best speakers in the party. An active church member and a person truly concerned about other human beings, Mrs. Horting was a logical selection. Although Secretary Horting fell on the political side of the Governor's cabinet, her merits were more than merely political. Just as Harry Shapiro had been active in the enactment of Pennsylvania's welfare legislation, Ruth Horting had contributed to the enactment of Pennsylvania's public assistance legislation. These two individuals had the rare opportunity to administer what they had helped to create.

THE MISSION OF PUBLIC ASSISTANCE

The policy of the Department of Public Assistance was to provide for human needs without reducing self-respect. The statement of legislative intent in the act creating the Department of Public Assistance identifies the state's desire to

> promote the welfare and happiness of all the people of the Commonwealth, by providing public assistance to all of its needy and distressed.; that assistance shall be administered promptly and humanely with due regard for the preservation of family life, and without discrimination on account of race, religion, or political affiliations; and that assistance shall be administered in such way and manner as to encourage self respect, self dependency and the desire to be a good citizen and useful to society.

The Department of Public Assistance included the Secretary and a staff of about 600 persons. A State Board of Public Assistance established policy and approved departmental rules and regulations. The staff was responsible for the distribution of relief and the supervision of county public assistance offices. Every county had an office of public assistance, composed of staff and a county board. Board members served without compensation and were responsible for establishing local board policy, hiring office personnel, and reviewing relief appeals.

The philosophy of the public assistance legislation was to ensure sensitivity to human needs by strong local involvement and to spread financial obligations so that poorer communities were not taxed beyond their capacity. The financial responsibility belonged to the state and federal government, while the determination of eligibility was left to the local communities to formulate according to their needs.

The public assistance program was divided into five categories: dependent children, the elderly, the blind, the permanently disabled, and all others in the general assistance category. Only the first four categories received matching federal funds; support for the general category came completely from state funds. For this reason, the department constantly sought to keep the general category at a minimum and applications were scrutinized to determine whether individuals could be placed in the federally assisted programs rather than in the general category.

The general assistance group was by far the most flexible. Unlike present trends, the old age category was actually shrinking at the time because of eligibility of a growing number of elderly for other retirement plans. The blind, disabled, and dependent children categories increased somewhat with the growing population. The general category was highly responsive to the economic conditions of the state; in times of high unemployment or large strikes, public assistance payments from the general category increased dramatically. Despite the unemployment compensation program directed by the Department of Labor and Industry, the unemployed were often in need of direct public assistance. Since delays were commonplace in processing unemployment compensation, workers needed public assistance until they received their benefits. Furthermore, in communities with large labor surpluses, unemployment compensation benefits frequently ceased before a person could find employment. Public assistance was often the only means of support for these people and their families.

ADMINISTRATIVE STYLE

Secretary Horting believed that it was important to remember the real people at the service end of the department. One of her first acts as Secretary was to visit all the county public assistance offices. Amazingly, this was the first time that a Secretary of Public Assistance had taken such a sensible step. Quite naturally, many county employees saw her action as a favorable indication of interdepartmental relations. Deputy Robert Wray and Bureau

71

Chiefs Carl Crowe, Edwin McMahon, and Chauncey Gunderman, accompanied Mrs. Horting; they addressed the staff during the day and the county boards in the evening explaining the responsibilities of their bureau.

Secretary Horting not only visited the staff, but also inspected the facilities. Since her department was responsible for these, she wanted to establish a clear visual image of the county offices. She compared office locations to case loads to assess their accessibility to applicants. The Department of Property and Supply was authorized to lease offices and make needed renovations, but the final decisions belonged to the Secretary of Public Assistance. She wanted to be as informed as possible in order to make decisions wisely.

Secretary Horting kept a copy of the public assistance act's legislative intent on her desk to remind her constantly of the people to be served. As the pre-inaugural study had highlighted, the state central office staff sometimes lost sight of the recipients of state aid. Because they had no direct contact with the people they were serving, it was easy to look at cases simply as statistics and data. Secretary Horting carried this reminder even further. Posing as man and wife, she and her deputy went to Lancaster County's public assistance office. They invented a story and went through the process of applying for public assistance; although the staff knew who they were, their application was processed as usual. The experience left a lasting impression on the Secretary. Years later she said that the humiliation applicants experience at the hands of the bureaucracy was enough to make her want to throw herself in a creek.

Secretary Horting was also very interested in professionalizing her staff. Many employees had years of department service and were presumably competent, according to the merit system. But despite the absence of patronage, few case workers were trained social workers. The department established a release-time program for employees to attend college classes for social work, a laudable first step toward professionalizing assistance services.

In an administration where scientific and social research was essential for effective programs, it was not surprising that Secretary Horting established a committee to define "a decent standard of living." The department used this standard to establish public assistance levels. Although research can contribute information for a definition, the actual establishment of the standard is a highly subjective and value-laden process. For this reason, the act of definition is by nature controversial, and by circumstance highly political. If the standard were set too high, the department would not have sufficient funds to meet all needs and ultimately would require additional revenues. If the standard were too low, there would be undue hardships on the individuals receiving public assistance. This is the dilemma in administrative decision-making: how much is too much and how little is too little? How stringent would a definition be before it caused more expensive social problems, such as crime, juvenile delinquency, and mental illness?

Clearly, the committee, chaired by Dr. Fairchild Woodberry charged to define "a decent standard of living" for the citizens of Pennsylvania was faced with serious decisions. The committee studied standards from the federal government and other states. Its report and standards were used not only in the Leader administration, but also in subsequent ones.

With respect to legislation, Secretary Horting recalled the recurring appropriation battles. Each biennium, the legislature appropriated funds to the Department of Public Assistance based on projected needs. Invariably the amounts allocated would be insufficient; the department would then concentrate its efforts on demonstrating the need for a deficiency appropriation. The Secretary found it difficult to impress the immediacy of the problem upon the legislators. Without state appropriation, the federal government would not contribute its part of the assistance payment and no checks could be paid to recipients. However, each biennium, in a familiar "Harrisburg photo-finish," the legislature would appropriate the funds just before the deadline. Secretary Horting proudly stated that the public assistance payments were never late.

Perhaps the most important legislation developed by the Department of Public Assistance and passed during the Leader administration was that providing nursing care as part of the public assistance program. In order to finance this new service, $3,000,000 was appropriated. In addition, pensions for the blind were increased.

The public assistance program was intended to maintain the needy as responsible citizens rather than to render them as objects of charity. Secretary Horting firmly believed in self-respect and responsibility; she felt that if the individuals on public assistance were supported completely, without obligation, they would learn to become completely dependent on society.

The lien provision was one means of ensuring responsibility. A person who owned property but was without income could receive assistance without having to sell the property. The department placed a lien for the amount of assistance on the property. The department did not bother the public assistance recipients while they were alive or still lived in the property. However, if they sold it or died, the department could collect. Secretary Horting stated that she could not see why the children, who in many cases neglected their parents in need, should receive that property. The lien provision had the effect of reducing public assistance to an interest free loan. This was particularly the case with the unemployed and striking workers. They usually removed the lien by repaying the assistance money, as soon as they were working again.

Migrant laborers working in Pennsylvania were often indigent. Efforts by the Department of Labor and Industry during the second half of Leader's administration increased awareness of the migrant laborer's poverty in all state departments. Secretary Horting participated in that effort and visited the migrant camps to see the children who were receiving assistance. Public assistance provided relief for dependent children when they were found, but provided only emergency grants for the adults, even though they were often in need. Migrant laborers were not eligible for public assistance in Pennsylvania, because they were not residents of the state. The rationale for ineligibility was that the migrants did not contribute to the general state fund, so why should they take from Pennsylvania tax payers just for passing through. They should obtain public assistance from their home state. Or so it was argued. Secretary Horting agreed with this policy. Tragically, in many cases, migrants were not eligible for public assistance in any state including their presumed state of residency, because they often met no state's residency requirements. They were, for all practical purposes, people without a country; their plight was a national problem.

Employees in the Department of Public Assistance often questioned Secretary Horting's position on the lien and residency requirements. Generally considered a liberal, she assumed a conservative stance on these two aspects of public assistance. She strongly believed that the original intent of the law was to foster responsibility, and that these policies furthered this intent.

Governor Leader did not mention public assistance in many of his speeches, and it was not a topic of much discussion in the press. Secretary Horting remarked that Governor Leader was more interested in mental health than he was in public assistance. He did attempt to obtain public assistance for individuals released from mental institutions. He was particularly concerned with those who had been institutionalized for a long time, and who had few, if any, relatives to assist them. However, public assistance regulations prohibited such payments.

The Governor recalled one conversation with Secretary Horting and her deputy, Mr. Wray. They discussed ways of providing assistance to the released mental patients, but Deputy Wray cited a regulation which prohibited every idea mentioned. Frustrated, the Governor put this idea aside, but he later regretted that he did not pursue the idea more stubbornly, even "a second, third, and fourth time."

One explanation for the relatively small gubernatorial involvement with the Department of Public Assistance was probably that it was tied closely to the federal regulations. It was also a civil service department which most others were not and had an established tradition of excellent non-partisan activity. The Governor wisely gave greater freedom to the strong departments, directed his efforts toward the weaker ones.

MERGER

Although the merger of the Department of Welfare and Public Assistance consolidated services to needy citizens, Secretary Horting disliked the consolidation. She felt strongly that the public assistance programs were important enough to warrant a separate department and should not be lost in the shadow of welfare. But the merger did come about and Secretary Horting became Commissioner of Public Assistance in the new department. To offset her demotion, she was given an increase in salary and remained a cabinet member. Ruth Horting later became Secretary of Public Welfare in the Lawrence administration.

The work in public assistance did move with the times. Leader's team in this field, as elsewhere, worked effectively to bring departmental operations into direct contact with individual needs. Research, effective oversight, responsible leadership, and professionalized staff were key attributes of this coordinated effort. Although the department had not been, like some, a bureaucratic nightmare, Leader and his staff continually looked for ways to improve existing service and ways to address new problem areas.

DEPARTMENT OF HEALTH

Governor Fine somewhat professionalized the Department of Health by establishing a merit system for employment in the department and appointing the first professional public health administrator as the Secretary of Health, Dr. Russell E. Teague. These changes and the statutory authority to reorganize the department followed the issuance of the Keystone Report by the American Public Health Association in 1948. This report was a comprehensive study of Pennsylvania's Department of Health; it set the direction for department improvements by both Governors Fine and Leader.

The Department of Health, established in 1905, had been plagued by the traditional political problems found in most departments of Pennsylvania state government. The post of Secretary of Health was customarily given to the governor's personal physician or to a physician who qualified as a friend of the party. Personnel appointments throughout this large department were made through the patronage system. The merit system, established by the Fine administration, was the first attempt to improve the severely criticized department operations. Perhaps no department demanded highly qualified professional employees more than this one.

Dr. Thomas Parran and Dr. James Crabtree, of the University of Pittsburgh, and Dr. Norman Topping, of the University of Pennsylvania, were Leader's highly qualified advisors in the area of health. Their section of the pre-inaugural study recommended continued implementation of the Keystone Report. They criticized the previous administration for its inadequate support of the Department of Health and for delays in implementing the recommendations of the American Public Health Association. They urged the Leader administration to implement a true merit system in the department immediately. The 1953 Chesterman Report had suggested the consolidation of the Departments of Health, Welfare, and Public Assistance, but Leader's advisors recommended a separate health department.

SELECTION OF THE SECRETARY

George Leader deviated from past political practices in the selection of his Secretary of Health. Not only did he appoint a non-resident, but also he chose a Republican—Dr. Berwyn F. Mattison. Dr. Mattison was not even a personal friend of George Leader. Leader selected him because of his qualifications and the recommendations of his health advisors, after an extensive search for candidates. Dr. Mattison recalled that his initial interviews for the position were not with the governor, but with David Randall, Dr. Parran, and Adolph Schmidt, a member of the State Advisory Health Board. The meeting was held at Mr. Schmidt's office at Mellon Bank in Pittsburgh. The Mellons were active supporters of improved health programs in Pennsylvania. The criteria for the selection of the Secretary of Health was first that the person be an M.D.; second, trained and experienced in public health; and third, be a competent administrator. Dr. Mattison possessed these qualifications. Previous to his appointment by Governor Leader, he had been the Director of the Health Department of Erie County in New York State; the county included the City of Buffalo.

Dr. Mattison remembered his first staff meeting when he addressed his staff to set the direction for his administration. Most of the employees had worked under the previous administration. He told them that if they could not see the connection between their daily work and public health, they should reexamine their reasons for being in the department. Dr. Mattison thought this was a fine way to motivate his employees; instead, he found his statement interpreted as the raising of the political axe to trim off the Republicans. After this misunderstanding was corrected, and competency not politics was established as the criterion for retention, morale improved. Personnel changes were made only where unqualified persons held positions. These persons were removed and qualified people hired to replace them according to a true merit system to which Governor Leader gave his full support.

Secretary Mattison's first task was to implement this merit system. In order to do this, it was necessary to replace the personnel director who had made political appointments in the previous administration. However, Secretary Mattison's actions were met with some resistance. Pressure came from Democratic leaders to continue the practices of patronage appointments. Indeed, despite occasional differences on issues and variations in support groups—a large common denominator of all political parties everywhere; that is the disposition in office, to regard said office—not as a public trust, but as an opportunity to play political games for purely partisan advantage. Leader did not see it that way. Politicians were not happy about losing control over any patronage positions since patronage was "the cement of the party."

The merit system established in the preceding administration had not been wholeheartedly supported by the Governor. Abuses had been overlooked. Political appointees still found their way onto the payroll, primarily through the misuse of temporary positions. An unqualified person would be placed in a position "temporarily" until a qualified person could be found. Often the search for that qualified person was delayed or forgotten and the political appointee remained in the position. A large number of superannuated persons, especially in high departmental positions was another problem. The directors of nursing and sanitation programs were well beyond retirement age. As those employees retired, Dr. Mattison, through extensive recruiting, filled the positions with highly qualified persons who gave new leadership. As in many other departments during the Leader administration, the Department of Health was reorganized to increase efficiency and to extend its services. The Bureau of Public Health Nursing was added to the department's field service bureaus.

PREVENTIVE MEDICINE

George Leader's concern for public health was as strong as his concern for programs for mental health, education for the handicapped, the well-being of the disabled, and the elderly, and other groups for whom he felt government was responsible. In his campaign, he promised "to give Pennsylvania the best public health program in the nation—a program in keeping with the skills and living standards of the state." The Governor explained in his speeches that the Department of Health had been established to eliminate typhoid, dysentery, cholera, tuberculosis, and other communicable diseases; and it had done well.

Nevertheless, the department could not be content simply to prevent new outbreaks of diseases which had been effectively reduced. Rather, the Department of Health had to confront and control new health hazards which were threatening the citizens of the State. The Governor wanted legislation and department involvement in the areas of air pollution, cancer and heart disease research, food and drug control, alcoholism, drug addiction, and radiation regulation and protection.

The Governor saw the department's role as one of prevention rather than cure. He said, "preventive medicine in public health demonstrates the highest level of a state's concern for its people by keeping them well and safeguarding the continuing health and strength of large groups of people, rather than the amelioration of the ills of individuals." As a farmer, George Leader was well educated in the benefits of preventive medicine in animals. Medical research on animals was far ahead of human medical research because there were fewer difficulties with experimentation with animals. The Governor knew that preventive measures, such as inoculations and sanitary conditions, were more profitable to the farmer than the curing of sick animals. George Leader brought this idea to the Department of Health and urged health professionals to develop methods of preventive medicine, so that more people would remain healthy. It was less expense for the state to prevent disease than to treat the sick, without even including the lost productivity of those who would normally have been working.

George Leader saw four stages in society's role of caring for its citizens. At the first level, society safeguards citizens from violence. At the next level, it provides adequate food and shelter for the needy. At the third level, the state provides medical care for citizens unable to care for themselves. The highest level is the one at which society develops preventive medicine and is concerned for the continuing health of the public, rather than only treating the sick. In the words of the Governor, "there is a swelling tide of public opinion against the economic and humanitarian nonsense of waiting until death or disability strikes before the community takes action in a health problem."

Dr. Mattison explained that this "swelling tide" came in the forms of increased federal aid for public health, U.S. Public Health Service leadership, and growing interest of various state public health and voluntary health agencies. The establishment of county health units was supported by many groups and recommended by the Keystone Report. The Department of Health encouraged the development of local health departments and supported legislation that provided funds for training local health workers. But the concept to extend health services was of little success. Only Allegheny County joined Philadelphia in home rule health programs. Since the county health units did not develop, the Department of Health opened six district offices, in order to provide more evenly distributed services.

Other legislative achievements sponsored by the administration in the area of health were: the codification and modernization of the communicable disease laws, a new dangerous drug act, legislation which permitted the State to care for non-indigent tuberculosis patients, and the acquisition of a tuberculosis hospital for the western part of the state. Since many of the legislative measures recommended in the Keystone Report had been enacted during the Fine administration, little new legislation was needed to improve the department's programs.

Two diseases, polio and tuberculosis, declined in Pennsylvania during the Leader administration. The newly discovered polio vaccine, developed by Dr. Jonas Salk at the University of Pittsburgh, had almost halted the spread of this crippling disease. Governor Leader presented Dr. Salk with the state's medal for meritorious service. George Leader pointed out that the polio vaccine was used throughout the state very quickly; by 1957, two-thirds of the children had been immunized. This was a great achievement, when one considers how many years were needed to immunize the population against diphtheria.

Tuberculosis had been reduced dramatically by the use of antibiotic drugs that facilitated home treatment rather than extended hospitalization. Early treatment also aided the fight against this long-dreaded disease. The improvements in tuberculosis treatment and the good working relationship between the various departments in Leader's administration enabled the Department of Health to turnover its unused beds in the tuberculosis hospitals to the Department of Welfare. They were given to mentally handicapped persons and thus reduced the long waiting lists for the state mental institutions.

The one area where politics often entered into Department of Health programs was in the streams. The Secretary of Health and the Secretary of Forest and Waters co-chaired the Sanitary Water Board, which was responsible for clean stream inspection and enforcement. Pennsylvania waters were of vital importance to many different interests. Transportation, commercial, industrial, residential, and recreational interests all placed demands on the water supply. Clean water was also essential for good health. When the Department of Health would discover someone dumping sewage or industrial wastes into a stream, it was not unusual for a local politician to come to the defense of the person violating the regulations arguing that no one has gotten sick before, so why stop now. Normal political procedure would have been for the Secretary of Health to receive a message from the Governor's office requesting the Secretary to reconsider any action to stop the pollution. Dr. Mattison recalled that when local politicians contacted the Governor, he would get a message telling him to enforce the regulations. Dr. Mattison said that it was fortunate that Dr. Maurice K. Goddard, another professional, co-chaired that board rather than a politician, because during the Leader administration, streams were inspected and regulations enforced.

In 1957, the American Public Health Association asked Dr. Mattison to become its executive director, a position he held for 13 years. One of his final acts as secretary was to approve the discharge of waste water from the nuclear reactor in Shippingport. This approval came after long and exhaustive studies. The department, under Secretary Mattison, had also developed regulations for the safe handling of radioactive materials in industry, business, and medicine. These regulations were used as a model by many other states when developing their regulations.

Dr. Charles Wilbar, Deputy Secretary of Health during the Fine and Leader administrations, succeeded Dr. Mattison as Secretary and held that position under Leader, Lawrence, and Scranton. Dr. Wilbar, a native of Pennsylvania, had been the head of the Department of Health in Hawaii before he returned to Pennsylvania to serve as Deputy Secretary of Health. Wilbar continued the work begun by his predecessor.

DEPARTMENT OF LABOR
AND INDUSTRY

Organized labor in Pennsylvania had not been happy with sixteen years of uninterrupted Republican dominance in Harrisburg. Republican administrations certainly had not earned a reputation for being pro-labor. Indeed, labor had been one of George Leader's staunch supporters during his gubernatorial campaign. The Governor viewed his election as an implied mandate to reverse the effects of sixteen years of Republican labor legislation and regulation. As to Leader's performance, Nelson McGeary, professor of political science at Penn State University, asserted unequivocally that Leader was the best friend in the Governor's seat that labor ever had.

Significant labor legislation had been passed during the Earle administration, including the creation of the Bureau of Employment Security. This occurred from 1935 to 1939, in a wave of reform legislation sometimes called the "Little New Deal." The Bureau of Employment Security was responsible for dispensing unemployment compensation benefits and conducting a placement service. Paul Smith,[1] who worked in the Workmen's Compensation Bureau, recalls that Governor Leader's Attorney General, Herbert Cohen, predicted that the administration's posture would be one of enforcement rather than of innovation in the area of labor legislation. Cohen felt that during the Earle administration, the General Assembly, of which he had then been a member, had enacted the necessary labor legislation. He felt the fault of Republicans was in their failure to implement and enforce that legislation. Minimum wage, unemployment compensation, workmen's compensation, and job safety laws were, to a considerable degree, debilitated by a lack of enforcement and by interpretations of law that consistently favored management.

To an extent, the task facing the Leader administration was thus one of enforcing old laws rather than creating new ones. However, Leader's administration also extended basic

---

[1]Paul Smith was Secretary of Labor and Industry under Governor Shapp.

labor laws to making them comparable to legislation in other industrial states.

THE PRE-INAUGURAL STUDY

The pre-inaugural study of the Department of Labor and Industry was conducted by R. Wallace Brewster, professor of political science at Penn State University. Brewster identified two basic problems in the department: personnel and budget procedures. These two areas had been, for practical purposes, out of the hands of the department secretary. The personnel problems derived mainly from political patronage which often resulted in unqualified and uncommitted employees. Brewster urged the establishment of a merit system, especially for referees, trial examiners, mediators, adjusters, and inspectors. The budgeting process seemed hampered by difficulties in communications; working arrangements with the comptroller needed clarification and definition. Brewster felt that eliminating these problems would put the department in a reasonably functioning condition.

SELECTION OF THE SECRETARY

When it came to the actual selection of the Secretary of Labor and Industry, Governor Leader listened to suggestions of labor leaders, whose choice for the position was Allen Sulcowe. He had been a career civil service worker in the Bureau of Employment Security and was known as a friend of labor. The Governor, however, had to weigh other considerations in forming a balanced cabinet. He had already appointed one labor person to his cabinet (Joe Kennedy in the Department of Mines and Mineral Industries) and the Democratic party leaders pressed Leader to find a cabinet post for John Torquato, the county chairman of Cambria County, who had been a loyal party leader and had the formidable support of David Lawrence of Pittsburgh. By appointing Torquato, George Leader placed a western Pennsylvania politician in his cabinet.

Allen Sulcowe remained an executive director of the Bureau of Employment Security, which employed approximately 70% of the department personnel. John Torquato was not very interested in the Bureau, probably because of its lack of patronage positions. As a recipient of federal funds for this program, the bureau was required to operate with civil service personnel. Torquato and Sulcowe were far apart in temperment and motivation, but they tolerated and respected each other. Torquato saw Sulcowe as a skilled administrator and Sulcowe understood that Torquato was a powerful politican whose support was essential to the department. They worked well together because of this mutual recognition.

LABOR LEGISLATION

The Bureau of Employment Security had been established in 1936 to assist unemployed workers. The department had two main objectives: unemployment compensation which was paid to eligible unemployed workers, and a job placement service to aid the unemployed. Employers paid into the unemployment insurance fund at a rate between 0.8% and 2.7% of their payroll, depending on the number of workers they employed.

Soon after George Leader became Governor, John Torquato informed him that the state unemployment insurance fund was approaching the "peril point"; the $300 million dollar level mandated by law to be maintained in the unemployment compensation fund. If the state's fund dropped to this base figure, all employers' contributions were automatically raised to the maximum, and payments to the unemployed were cut by one-third. Leader blamed the Republicans for the depleted unemployment compensation fund and called for immediate legislative measures to alleviate the problem. George Leader stressed that he did not want the fund to reach the "peril point" because it would place an unfair burden on business and industry and would counteract his program for industrial development. No company would want to locate in a state where they would pay the maximum percentage for unemployment compensation because of prior fund mismanagement.

Leader needed a sound fund before he could increase un-employment benefits. The Governor planned to raise the amount of weekly benefits and extend the length of time for payments. George Leader often spoke of the need for such legislation, stressing that the Democratic party was respon-sible for the initial unemployment legislation and now it should push ahead to liberalize the laws. After the House passed the amendments, the Republican-controlled Senate took no action on them. Governor Leader intensified his ver-bal attacks on the Republicans claiming that their sixteen years of rule had thwarted the labor program and that it was time for them to follow the popular mandates of the people who had placed the Democrats in power. The Governor men-tioned the need for these increased benefits often in his speeches, appealing to the citizens to urge their legislators to enact the increases.

His tactics found some success for the employment com-pensation fund was strengthened. In February of 1956, the Senate passed the unemployment compensation amend-ments; the minimal weekly benefits were increased from $30 to $35 and the number of eligible weeks extended from 26 to 30. This legislation gave unemployed Pennsylvanians the highest benefits in the nation.

No less significant to labor were the accompanying amendments to the worker's compensation legislation. The Governor often pointed out how absurd it was to have only certain diseases listed as occupational diseases, while other equally serious diseases incurred through employment were not covered by the law. It also seemed cruel negligence to provide compensation to disabled workers only for 700 weeks. What happened to the worker and his family after 700 weeks: did his disability disappear? The amendments to the occupational disease legislation extended the definition of compensable job-related diseases and extended the period of compensation to injured workers through the rest of their lives, if necessary.

Nevertheless, providing benefits for the unemployed was not the main objective of Leader's administration. This was the negative, or compensatory aspect. His goal was full em-ployment; for with it, every one would prosper, labor and management. But full employment was not an easily obtainable goal, for both the Governor and the public realized that progress requires more than rhetoric. In 1955, his speeches resounded with the same themes: humanize the mental health programs; educate the handicapped children; and find jobs for the unemployed. Repetition of these themes did not weary or bore those who had families and friends in these categories of need, rather the Governor's words were a ray of hope. His accomplishments in all three areas prove that Leader's words were not merely idle political rhetoric.

A positive verbal approach to the unemployment problems was not new; to create new jobs was an obvious sensible solution for the problem of labor surplus; but, unlike past administrations, George Leader actually made some progress in that direction. He advocated economic development and had legislation introduced which created the Pennsylvania Industrial Development Authority (see Department of Commerce). This program produced a different attitude in the Department of Labor and Industry, especially in the Bureau of Employment Security, where like the public assistance staff, they found themselves on the negative side of the social service spectrum. They doled out money as a stopgate to despair. Leader thought positively; although the administration provided decent benefits for the unemployed, it was more important to find them work so that unemployment compensation was not needed. As the Governor's industrial development program began to produce results, the attitude of the bureau became more positive, and morale improved.

LABOR'S SUPPORT FOR THE GOVERNOR'S PROGRAMS

There were four major labor organizations during the Leader administration: the A F of L, headed by Joseph McDonough; the CIO, headed by Harry Boyer; the Railway Brotherhood, headed by Charles Sludden; and the Mine Workers, led by Lester Thomas. At Leader's invitation, the labor leaders often met with the Governor in the mansion. A solid respect for the Governor and his programs developed among them. The Governor identified with labor and often compared his job as Governor to the role of the labor leader. Leader actively solicited labor's support for his programs such as special education for the handicapped, mental health, higher education, labor legislation, and especially his tax program.[2] Leader's promise to enact a broad-based tax, instead of a wage or sales tax, led to one of the longest legislative sessions in the state's history. The tax battle tended to dwarf the progressive programs which the administration achieved. Critics of the administration believe that Leader's biggest mistake was holding out against the sales tax for so long; others characterize his resistance as justified. The tax battle left an indelible mark on the administration; Leader lost the support of many Democratic leaders. However, as Henry Leader pointed out, the tax battle kept the legislature in session long enough to pass what was probably the most humanitarian legislation ever enacted in Pennsylvania.

Because of Pennsylvania's constitutional provision that everyone be taxed equally, a graduated income tax, like the federal income tax was not constitutional. The Fine administration had enacted a 1% sales tax, and the Republicans were set on maintaining the sales tax as the primary means of generating revenue. George Leader considered that tax regressive, claiming that those who could afford it least were carrying the burden of the tax. Instead, Leader favored a broad-based tax, which evolved into the "classified income tax." To assure the constitutionality of the tax, wages were to be taxed at a lower percentage than income derived from investments. Since the Republicans were already committed to a sales tax, the Governor had difficulty gathering support for his tax package. Because many people prefer to pay taxes in pennies rather than dollars, the Governor's tax scheme was not appreciated immediately. The administration undertook an extensive educational program to show that the average Pennsylvanians would pay less with the income tax then they would through the sales tax. Organized labor was won over and added its support of the tax package. But all that energy was of no avail, for the Governor had to sign the

---

[2]For a more complete analysis of Leader's tax program and the role played by labor, see Elias Bertram Silverman's Ph.D. dissertation at Penn State: "Constraint On Innovation: a Classified Tax for Pennsylvania."

3% sales tax, thus breaking his promise. In effect, the Governor won the battle over his tax package with the people, but lost where it really counted, in the legislature.

FAIR EMPLOYMENT PRACTICE COUNCIL

The Fair Employment Practice Council bill had been kicked around the Pennsylvania Legislature for about ten years. This political football was supported by the Democratic minority, and opposed by the Republican majority. This civil rights legislation would have prohibited discrimination in employment because of race, color, creed, ancestry, or national origin. While George Leader was in the state Senate, he had supported efforts to establish the Fair Employment Practice Council. Leader often referred to the FEPC bill as, "legislation which will declare it to be the public policy of this Commonwealth that individual competence, and not race, religion, or national origin shall be the prerequisite for employment in Pennsylvania."

Early in his administration, the Democrats, now in the majority in the House, again introduced the FEPC bill where it passed quickly. But the Republican majority in the Senate defeated the bill in committee. The Senate leaders were not swayed by the Governor's pleas for the bill's passage and as the prospect of another defeat neared, the Governor strengthened his statements and asked citizens to urge their Senators to support the important civil rights bill. In May, the Governor called a conference in Harrisburg of various supporters of the FEPC. This strong demonstration of support for the provision was enough to influence the Senate to act.

Responding to increased public support which the Governor was obtaining for the FEPC measure, the Senate revived the bill in committee but expressed its independence by adding age to the provisions of the bill. The Governor warned, "the great danger is that we permit ourselves to believe that with a single word or phrase added to the FEPC measure we can master a perplexing problem of this kind and actually leave undone the long arduous task before us."

The Governor went a step further in June and invited the labor leaders, civil rights leaders, and other supporters of the

FEPC to a luncheon in the mansion to discuss strategies for ensuring its passage. The group drafted a statement addressed to the Senate endorsing the FEPC legislation without the age provision and urged its immediate enactment.

This public show of strength on the part of the Governor to impress the Republicans was enough to influence the bill's passage, but with the age provisions still attached. Leader was not pleased with the bill because of the age provision but he still claimed a victory stating that the state finally had a FEPC program. But the Senate delayed again in approving the persons named to the council.

LEADER'S SUPPORT FOR LABOR SAFETY

Legislation was not the administration's only tool as it worked diligently for labor's interest. Safety regulations had often been ignored during the four preceding administrations. George Leader saw the role of his administration as the enforcer of the worker's rights and emphasized strict inspection of work places and adherence to safety regulations.

John (Gerry) Dwyer was appointed as director of the Bureau of Inspection, where he did an outstanding job enforcing safety regulations. The railroad industry is an example of the administration's efforts. At the end of the Fine administration, rail workers obtained judicial action to require the state to enforce sanitation regulations mandated by federal law. The new Democratic administration quickly obeyed the court order and began enforcing the rail worker's sanitation regulations. Full crew regulations, often overlooked in the past, were enforced as well. Governor Leader compared the full crew requirements for railroad employees to the airline industry, where no one would think of flying an airplane without a co-pilot for emergencies. On the trains, a sole engineer was considered sufficient. In fact, "full crew" requirements were often characterized by anti-labor critics as "featherbedding."

George Leader proudly stated that "we've taken safety out of politics—and that means a safety order can no longer be set aside by a telephone call to someone with political influence." To achieve this, the administration placed all 160 state inspectors under civil service. In addition, the inspectors received special training, enabling them to inspect all five safety factors instead of only one. Thus, one inspector could complete a site inspection rather than waiting for five inspectors. Moreover, when there were safety violations, they were reported. The increase in reported violations is attributable both to the use of civil service inspectors and the inspectors' knowledge that their reports would not be changed by their supervisors. John Dwyer credits these achievements to the Governor's total support. Dwyer never had to fear that the Governor would sanction a violation for political reasons.

THE CHICAGO SCHOOL FIRE

Late in 1958, a tragic fire swept through a Chicago school building, killing over 100 children. Despite the lateness in his term of office, Governor Leader took immediate drastic action to ensure that this tragedy in Chicago would not be repeated in Pennsylvania. He ordered the Bureau of Inspection to check for adequate fire escapes, fire doors, and stairways in every school building. The bureau had complete authority to close down any school which did not comply with the fire safety standards; there were many that did not. The school boards did not welcome the expense involved in providing proper safety. The inspection resulted in the permanent closing of some schools and the instruction of Pennsylvania's school children in buildings prepared for emergencies.

TORQUATO DUMPED

George Leader fired John Torquato in January 1957. The actual causes for dismissal are somewhat obscure. The Governor felt that John Torquato had done a fine job in his first two years. As one observer pointed out, he was a good soldier who followed his captain's orders. Yet others suggest that he was probably one of several Democratic politicians discontent with George Leader.

A growing disenchantment with the stubborn young Governor, who kept his campaign promises with a crusading fervor, developed in the Democratic party. To varying degrees, party leaders were displeased with Leader. Toward the midpoint of his administration, after the long tax battle, Lieutenant Governor Furman demonstrated his discontent by slowly breaking with the Leader administration and laying the groundwork for his own unsuccessful bid for the Governorship two years later. The Governor and Lieutenant Governor grew so far apart that Furman was part of the administration in title only.

Disagreements emerged in the party, especially in the Senate where the Democratic Senators had been accustomed to being in the minority and did not have the power of a majority enjoyed by House members and the executive branch. They were accustomed to Republican control and were not eager to blindly support the Governor whom they criticized for his political tactics, more accurately, his refusal to play political games. According to a reliable source, Senator Joseph Barr, the Democratic State Chairman, told the Governor in the midst of the tax battle that campaign promises were not binding contracts, but only a political tool to win elections. Leader disagreed. Leader had also alienated local politicians by successfully eliminating patronage from many state government positions. Torquato was one of the politicians who disliked Leader's resistance to traditional Pennsylvania party politics; their disagreement became obvious.

Discontent climaxed in arguments over a "special payroll" in the Department of Labor and Industry. Stories were circulated in the press and around the Capitol about Torquato's "special payroll" that was full of "ghost-workers." It was even rumored that clergymen were on this payroll. Speculation persisted, and the Governor felt compelled to act. He asked Torquato to show him the alleged payroll.

The payroll was drawn from a legitimate fund accumulated through the collection of fines in the Bureau of Employment Security. These fines were neither state nor federal funds, but were intended to be used by the bureau to hire persons to investigate possible unemployment compensation fraud. Most people on the payroll were holdovers from the

92

Fine administration, however, Torquato added several other persons. Paul Smith, Director of the Bureau of Employment Compensation, was responsible for providing work assignments for the investigators and preparing their expense accounts. He admitted that some of those on the special payroll were serious workers while others were only serious about the money they received. As publicity mounted about the special payroll, Torquato became inappropriately flippant about it, apparently enjoying the publicity.

The special account and a letter to the Governor implying the Governor was using political favoritism in his administration brought the Governor to the drastic action of requesting John Torquato's resignation. The Governor said bluntly, "due to the fact that we are not in accord as to the mode of operation of the Department of Labor and Industry, I am requesting that you submit your resignation."

Torquato had done nothing blatantly illegal, but he had disregarded the Governor's directives to eliminate political excesses from state government. George Leader would not tolerate any irregularities in the use of public funds for which he felt personally responsible. The Governor informed his cabinet that the Torquato incident should stand as a warning to the rest of them that he would not stand for any irregularities in the conduct of their departments.

SELECTION OF THE NEW SECRETARY

George Leader appointed Deputy Secretary Weisberg as Acting Secretary of Labor and Industry. Labor again suggested Allen Sulcowe for the position, but Leader searched outside of the department, even out of the state, and selected William Batt, whom he had originally asked to be Secretary of Commerce. "Bill" Batt was the son of an industrialist and a graduate of Harvard. He was interested in economic development and the plight of the unemployed. Batt had written an article on economic development, and Leader used the fact that the Secretary of Labor and Industry was a member of the PIDA board as a way of enticing Batt to take the position. He had twice turned down offers to become Secretary of

Commerce, because he felt obligated to continue the project of industrial development in Toledo, Ohio. He accepted the invitation to be Secretary of Labor and Industry, because he felt the Toledo project had developed sufficiently and could continue its momentum under other leadership.

Bill Batt was very different in many ways from Torquato. Where Torquato was a politician, Batt was a professional. His subordinates recalled that when the party sent tickets to the department for political events, Batt wanted to know nothing about them. He brought to the department his interest in economic development, in retraining of the unemployed and dedication to improving the worker's situation, especially the unemployed. He later served under President Kennedy as Director of the Area Redevelopment Authority.

Like George Leader, Batt possessed a reservoir of ideas and a tireless championing of good causes. His subordinates often criticized Batt for his crusades claiming that they took up too much of his time, since the people they helped represented only a small part of the labor force. This fact, however, impressed Governor Leader, who saw the role of government to help those unable to help themselves. Leader supported Batt and was pleased with his work. Batt emphasized three programs: rehabilitation of the handicapped, minimum wage for women and children, and state aid for migrant workers.

REHABILITATION OF HANDICAPPED WORKERS

In 1949, Dr. Howard Rush, in an article in the *New York Times* described Pennsylvania as having one of the country's worst vocational rehabilitation programs. Although limited progress was made in the early 1950's, unprecedented improvement was achieved during the Leader administration. Two committees were formed; the Governor's Commission on Rehabilitation and the Governor's Committee on the Employment of the Handicapped were composed of citizens who encouraged the employment of handicapped and disabled workers.

The efforts of the Department of Labor and Industry's Bureau of Rehabilitation were rewarded when the federal government recognized Pennsylvania for having placed the greatest number of rehabilitated and handicapped workers in employment for two consecutive years. The bureau placed 5,794 workers in 1957, and 6,537 in 1958. The 1958 achievement is significant because there was an economic recession that year and Pennsylvania's unemployment rate had reached 10 percent.

The administration assisted the handicapped and disabled workers even further by being the first state to revise its state building code to require access ramps for the handicapped in new buildings. Governor Leader explained, "this vital problem of building accessibility will eliminate the bottleneck in the total rehabilitation process; for if a physically handicapped person cannot gain access to his place of employment, he is, for all practical purposes, not fully rehabilitated."

Contrary to the popular conception, the rehabilitation program was not a costly "hand-out" program. Governor Leader was quick to point out that, even leaving humanitarian considerations aside, "the rehabilitation and employment of the physically handicapped is economically sound. According to the records of the Bureau of Rehabilitation, a worker put back in a job not only becomes financially independent, but pays enough income tax within the course of five or six years to return to the government the cost of his rehabilitation."

Mary Jane Leader, the Governor's wife, suggested to Bill Batt that the department assist the sheltered workshops for the handicapped around the state. She had been impressed by the accomplishments of a sheltered workshop in Carlisle. Subsequently, the department did assist the workshops by providing transportation for the handicapped workers and by giving assistance in obtaining contracts for simple work for their clients.

At the end of October in 1958, Governor Leader dedicated the new State Rehabilitation Center in Johnstown, the first of its kind in the nation. All the services for the handicapped and disabled were provided in one institution, including facilities for job training.

THE MINIMUM WAGE STRUGGLE

Three classes of workers not covered by any state or federal minimum wage law in Pennsylvania were women and children in the retail, laundry, and hotel industries. Secretary Batt began a campaign to include these workers in minimum wage regulations. He chose Elizabeth Johnston, an expert in the area of minimum wage, to direct the Women and Children Bureau. Leader's administration met strong opposition to this appointment, since this directorship was a traditional political plum reserved for a faithful party member. Though a native of Pennsylvania, Johnston had been working out of state when Batt selected her. After some political struggle, she was confirmed and worked diligently to upgrade the wage levels of these workers.

The federal minimum wage law provided that any group of workers excluded under federal regulations should be covered by state law. Thus, new legislation to extend coverage was not necessary. Three committees were established to study the situation of each group; in each case they determined that a minimum wage should be established. The department successfully established minimum wage levels despite court battles to reverse the committees' decisions. Secretary Batt regretted that one of the side effects of the minimum wage requirements was the loss of jobs in the retail trade stores, since many businesses switched to self-service rather than pay the increased cost of labor.

MIGRANT LABORERS

During the first two years of the administration, efforts were made to improve the living conditions of migrant laborers who worked for periods throughout the state. These efforts were intensified in the second two years by Secretary Batt who had the Governor's full support to do everything possible to improve the plight of these workers. Pennsylvania's fruit and vegetable growers relied on seasonal labor to harvest their crops. The state's agriculture was partially dependent on 40,000 seasonal workers; 30,000 Pennsylvanians and 10,000 migrant workers from the South and Puerto Rico comprised the seasonal labor force.

Seasonal laborers have been around for many years and their problems were not new. Nor were the attempts to help these people new. At the turn of the century, various church groups worked to improve the plight of the migrant farm laborers, who at that time were Eastern Europeans. In the 1950's most of the migrants were southern blacks and Puerto Ricans. Their needs were tremendous. They had very poor housing, little or no health care, low wages, few educational opportunities for their children, oppressive and often unjust working environments, no employment security, and minimal community services. Moreover, they were ineligible for public assistance and often were in trouble with law enforcement agencies.

The Department of Labor and Industry, through its Bureau of Inspections, began a program of safety inspections in the migrant camps and closed those camps which did not comply. Regulations pertaining to crew leaders who brought the migrants into the state were enforced as well. These efforts were intensified and increased by Secretary Batt in the last two years of the administration.

The attitude of many people was that the workers were needed and therefore, they were tolerated. The growers would house the laborers for as short a time as possible and the communities would endure the invasion of the migrants only because it was necessary for their local economy.

The conditions in which the migrants lived and worked have been well documented by many authors. As one person in the Department of Labor and Industry put it, "the animals often lived in better facilities than the migrants. The migrants were sometimes quartered in old chicken coops, sheds, barns, and often without indoor plumbing."

The Governor established an advisory board of concerned citizens to revise the thirty-year old regulations for migrant housing. The new regulations required hot and cold running water, refrigeration, a cooking area, and a minimum number of square feet per person. John Dywer, head of the Bureau of Safety, increased state inspections of the labor camps. When the owners did not comply with the regulations, the bureau closed the camps. Many growers were not pleased with the increased enforcement and new regulations because it was often expensive to bring the migrant camps into compliance with the regulations. Some growers chose to buy automated crop harvesters rather than repair the camps.

The Governor tempered the administration's campaign for decent conditions and services for the migrants by pointing out that not all were bad, that many growers did provide decent housing for migrant laborers. His campaign was against those inconsiderate persons who maintained sub-human living conditions.

Not every migrant labor camp was sub-standard, and many passed inspection after only minor repairs. Governor Leader suggested that Secretary Batt use "the carrot as well as the stick," by giving an award to the best maintained migrant labor camps as an incentive.

However, Secretary Batt saw housing improvements as only one of the many reforms needed. To address the other problems facing the migrant laborers, Secretary Batt formed an inter-departmental committee, composed of representatives from the Departments of Labor and Industry, Health, Public Assistance, Forest and Waters, State Police, Justice, Public Instruction, and Agriculture. This committee met often and developed specific programs to assist the migrants.

Among these programs were improvements in housing conditions, inspection of vehicles transporting migrants through the state, provisions for x-rays and blood tests, encouragement of religious services, payment of emergency grants from the Department of Public Assistance and the establishment of day care programs for children operated by the Department of Public Assistance and Welfare. In addition, the inter-departmental committee made state government agencies more sensitive to the problems and needs of migrants in the state.

Another product of Batt's efforts was the establishment of an interstate commission on migrant laborers among the eastern states. Representatives from a number of states met to discuss migrant problems and to formulate standards and procedures applicable to all migrant workers in the state. The major obstacle complicating migrant labor problems was the difference between the states' rules and regulations. Batt felt that these regulations would ameliorate the plight of the migrants. Although the states were not ready to adopt such a program, later federal migrant labor regulations can be traced to this interstate committee chaired by William Batt.

BUREAU OF MEDIATION

The reorganization of state government not only rearranged departments and facilitated the management of Pennsylvania's executive branch, it also helped identify problem areas. One such area was the Bureau of Mediation. The staff of this bureau was available to assist labor and industry in the settlement of strikes. The director of the bureau had a staff of mediators scattered throughout the state. These were political positions and were often considered "ghosts" because many appeared only to be paid and then some were upset because they had to appear in person to receive their pay checks.

Over the years the state mediators had lost much of their influence because of the political nature of their positions. The federal government also had mediators whose services were more often sought because of the professional status of their positions. The staff of the Office of Administration identified this weakness and late in the administration, John Ferguson, Secretary of Administration, requested Charles Douds to come to Pennsylvania to head the Bureau of Mediation. Douds had been with the National Labor Relations Board for 15 years, first in Pittsburgh and then as regional director in New York.

Douds became the Director of the Bureau in the fall of 1958 a few months before George Leader left office. He subsequently served as the director of the Bureau until 1969 under Governors Lawrence, Scranton, and Shafer. During the years he was director, Douds established three regional offices in Pittsburgh, Philadelphia, and Hazleton and obtained civil service status for the mediators. Consequently the status of the state mediators rose and they were better able to serve labor and industry along with the federal mediators.

THE 1958 RECESSION

In 1958, Pennsylvania found itself in a recession that affected most of the nation's industrial areas. Unemployment reached an alarming 10 percent. In these times, the Leader administration demonstrated its sensitivity to public needs and its determination to use government to improve economic conditions. Many people lamented the recession and waited for it to pass. However, George Leader and his advisors were not passive. Bill Batt advocated the new dealish expedient of accelerating public work projects in an effort to ease unemployment. The Governor totally supported the plan and told his cabinet not only that the job development project had top priority but that they should "fire anyone dragging their heels or giving only half-hearted support to this program." The administration funded a series of public work projects totalling $30,000,000 to create jobs. Like Roosevelt's P.W.A., Leader's advisors believed that an industry that employed construction workers stimulated other industry by the purchase of heavy materials. This, in turn, stimulated their production. Each department of the administration was polled to identify approved projects that were scheduled for construction the following year. Those in the advanced stages of preparation were begun immediately; other projects still in various stages of planning were accelerated, with construction beginning well ahead of schedule.

The Governor and his staff promoted the public works doctrine at the local governments level. The Governor participated in many seminars throughout the state that were designed to acquaint local government officials with the concept and explain ways to accelerate their own public works projects. Bill Batt also advanced the idea at the National Governor's Conference. Secretary Batt reported that the public works concept was well received, as far as verbal reaction was concerned, especially by the industrial states hardest hit by the recession; however, he found no evidence of similar action. In his view, no state launched a campaign similar to Pennsylvania's.

Did the public works acceleration program actually help the state during the recession? People near the Governor felt that it did help ease the effect of the recession in Pennsylvania. A few felt that the reports were somewhat exaggerated because some of the public works projects would have been begun anyway in 1958. Others believed that the program's effects were difficult to measure, nevertheless, most agreed that it had a positive impact on the state. The same debate had attended the assessment of government spending during the New Deal. Evidences of impact of such matters will always be filtered through the peculiar eye-glasses of the political philosophy and economic theories of the beholder. Of primary significance is Leader's and Batt's choice of action over inaction; and their own commitment to alleviating poverty and distress.

THE AGING

Governor Leader had opposed the inclusion of age in the FEPC legislation because he felt that the problem of aging was separate and distinct. During the political struggle over the FEPC bill, Governor Leader addressed the General Assembly concerning the problems of the older workers and requested the legislature to authorize the formation of a study commission. An advisory board was formed to study these problems of the older workers and to make recommendations. In his charge to this board, the Governor further instructed them to identify any problems confronting all senior citizens. In 1957, the Governor enlarged the administration's efforts for the elderly by appointing a Governor's Committee on the Aging that worked closely with the inter-departmental committee on aging. In many of his speeches, Leader repeatedly emphasized the problems of the growing elderly population. Early aware of new realities, he emphasized that the situation would not improve—or go away—but would only worsen if attention of the state and federal government was not directed to the problems of the older citizens. He anticipated the now obvious fact that because the aged constitute an increased portion of the population, institutional and financial problems would be expanded many fold.

Chapter 4

Natural Resources

DEPARTMENT OF FOREST
AND WATERS

The vast natural wealth of the North American continent led to the early 19th century belief that these resources were infinite. Under the spell of this misconception, exploitation, waste, and reckless mining of land and forest seemed insignificant. America's resources appeared inexhaustiable, for infinity minus anything remains — infinity.

Reality suddenly caught up with the delusion. Buffalo herds thinned; the passenger pigeon which once clouded the sky was declared extinct. In 1890, the Bureau of Census officially declared that the frontier had vanished and with it the delusion of infinite resources. The vision changed to one of plenty, i.e., an abundance which nonetheless dictated prudence and conservation, and consideration of future generations. At the turn of the century, there was no sense of the imminent exhaustion of natural resources, like the "energy crunch" has produced today.

Pennsylvania gave conservation one of its best names and statesmen, Gifford Pinchot. This was appropriate, for Pennsylvania historically has been the ground for collision between forces of resource exploitation and conservationist social responsibility, of reckless versus prudent use. The Quakers, the Pennsylvania Dutch, and the "plain people" were among those whose cultures nurtured this prudent use. An early "bread-basket colony" agriculture lent a conservationist bias to the state's public policy. Husbandry dictates conservation; a farmer destroys his soil only from ignorance — not intent.

Pennsylvania had forests on its hills, and coal below its surface. Historically, coal and wood were favorite targets for some called "the Robber Barons" the artists of strip-and-scram and cut-and-run. Both the reckless and the prudent had their legitimate interests, and their political allies. Often, the Commonwealth was the stage for conflict between the private and the public good; between short-term and long-term conceptions of wealth and profit. Leader's administration worked consistently to balance long-term benefits for both private citizen and society.

Approximately 52% of Pennsylvania is forest land; two million acres of which are state forests. Pennsylvania is also blessed with extensive waterways; these were very influential in shaping Pennsylvania's development as an industrial state. The Department of Forest and Waters was founded in 1923 by Governor Gifford Pinchot, the "first American Forester." Previously, forests had been managed by the Division of Forests in the Department of Agriculture. In the 1920's, forestry was a new concept to Americans accustomed to using apparently unlimited resources. The practice of "cut out and get out" was common. Pinchot advocated the wise use and renewal of natural resources for the benefit of all the citizens of Pennsylvania.

SELECTION OF THE SECRETARY
OF FOREST AND WATERS

George Leader was determined to find a secretary for the Department of Forest and Waters, who naturally would care about Pennsylvania's natural resources, but also have the knowledge and ability to protect and renew those resources. For this reason, George Leader resisted his party's pressure to appoint politically-oriented John Torquato as Secretary of Forest and Waters. Instead of searching for candidates within the party, Leader turned to professional foresters. Dr. Maurice Goddard[1], President of the Pennsylvania Forestry

---

[1]Secretary Goddard held the position of Secretary of Forest and Waters until it became the Department of Environmental Resources. He continued as its director until 1979, serving under five governors; Leader, Lawrence, Scranton, Shafer, and Shapp. He has a truly remarkable record of highly qualified public service.

Association and Director of the School of Forestry of Pennsylvania State University had exactly the qualifications Leader desired in his Secretary. Maurice Goddard was a graduate of the Universities of Maine and California; he joined the Penn State faculty in 1935 and became director of the School of Forestry in 1953. He was also active in many local and national forestry associations. Goddard was one of the undisputed professionals in Leader's cabinet. A registered independent, Goddard's political affiliations were more acceptable to the Democrats than some of Leader's Republican cabinet appointees.

As a forester, Maurice Goddard admired the efforts of Governor Pinchot, who had directed the forest commission under President Theodore Roosevelt. Governor Leader also respected Pinchot both for his conservation programs, and for his well run administration while Governor of Pennsylvania. This shared admiration for Pinchot created a strong bond between Leader and Goddard; both adhered, as Goddard expressed it, to Pinchot's concept of "use without abuse."

As a result of the pre-inaugural study and his own forestry experience the new Secretary was already familiar with many of the department's problems. As in other departments, unqualified personnel was a prime concern. The department had been established and operated on a professional basis by Governor Pinchot, who initiated forest management practices in Pennsylvania. In the intervening years, however, hiring practices had become political; and the county chairmen influenced personnel selection. Goddard saw himself as a professional doing a professional job; a workforce hired completely by the patronage system did not appeal to him, especially in a field where conservation practices were so crucial. A dramatic example of the negative quality of Pennsylvania's reputation in employment is the fact that only one of the 50 graduates of Penn State's School of Forestry had accepted a position in the department. The rest went to neighboring states where employment options were more attractive and more secure; since the department had no merit system and shamefully low salaries.

Goddard firmly believed that the three requisites for an effective organization were: the properly qualified personnel;

good programs; and adequate funds. Achieving these objectives in order ensured that public money was not wasted by unqualified personnel trying to develop programs. Secretary Goddard followed his plan. He removed employees from the patronage system and fired unqualified personnel, developed a specific program, and found the funds to implement it. The Pennsylvania state park system is Goddard's most notable accomplishment using this plan.

Secretary Goddard did not do wholesale firing in the department because in most cases the personnel were competent foresters. Many of the employees in the field had worked in the department since the Pinchot administration, displaced temporarily during the Earle administration. Since economic conditions of the Commonwealth in 1955 were not good, there were few vacancies caused by Republican employees leaving. Secretary Goddard strongly supported the executive civil service and was foresighted enough to require all his professional civil service employees to take examinations, rather than simply receiving that status by virtue of their position. Since the executive board civil service was not a law and might be temporary, Goddard required his employees to take the examinations, then, years later when the merit system became law, no one could argue that they obtained their positions for political reasons. Although Goddard would have liked to have the whole department under civil service, only positions requiring college-trained personnel were under the merit system. Those who failed the examination were not rehired. The remaining employees formed a strong group of professional employees to carry out Goddard's programs.

THE GAS AND OIL LEASES

The pre-inaugural study, done by William Schulz, professor of law at the University of Pittsburgh, cited several areas requiring attention. The most pressing, aside from personnel, was that of the gas and oil leases. The previous administration had hired a consultant to advise the department on the leasing of gas and oil rights on state forest lands and the leasing of those lands for gas storage. Alden Foster had established a working system to place leases in order and systematically collect revenues. Schulz recommended that more attention be paid to these leases and that plans be drawn for leasing exhausted wells for gas storage, since Pennsylvania gas wells were not long-term producers. The Leader administration hired Dr. Calhoun, a professor of engineering at Penn State University, as the department's consultant on gas and oil. Under his direction, a new Division of Minerals was established to handle the gas and oil leases. The development of a natural gas storage system was an economical way to ensure that the state would have adequate supplies of natural gas during the winter months. Storage tanks and additional pipelines to bring gas from out of state were too expensive. Besides their utility to the state's residents and industries, these underground storage sites on state land brought additional revenue to the state, even after the natural gas wells were exhausted.

THE HURRICANES: A DRAMATIC TEST OF POLICY AND PROGRAM

In August 1955, only seven months after George Leader took office, Hurricanes Connie and Diana hit the state within a few days of each other and caused extensive damage in eastern Pennsylvania, especially the Pocono Mountains. One hundred and one persons were killed, and damage to roads, streams, bridges, and personal property exceeded 70 million dollars. The administration directed its attention to the flood stricken area: the Departments of Forest and Waters, Highways, Health, Welfare, Public Assistance, and Military Affairs, in conjunction with the State Police and Civil Defense, utilized every available relief program to rescue stranded persons and to begin clean-up operations. Thousands of children were stranded at summer camps in the flood area; state, federal, and private agencies cooperated in the evacuation of children from areas isolated by flooding. Because the area had been declared a disaster area, federal relief was available. Nevertheless, the destruction of roads, bridges, and streams was so extensive that extraordinary measures were necessary to finance reconstruction. Within a month the General Assembly passed a temporary one cent tax on gasoline and cigarettes which the administration had requested to pay for repairing and rebuilding highways and clearing streams. Many Department of Forest and Waters employees worked for the duration of the administration in the stricken area, clearing the streams and forests.

Unbelievably, hurricane Ione hit Pennsylvania in October of the same year, again flooding the eastern part of the state. Fortunately, Ione was not as destructive as the two earlier hurricanes.

The impact of these natural disasters on the administration was evident. Governor Leader declared that he was making flood control a major concern because floods directly affected flooded areas, and indirectly affected other citizens socially and economically. Leader explained that his administration had launched a concerted campaign to protect the people from the "disastrous ravages of floods." In November 1955, he charged the State Planning Board with the responsibility of studying flood control throughout the State and recommending flood control projects to the Department of Forest and Waters. He also formed a Flood Committee to consider flood insurance, so that Pennsylvania could find financial protection from future floods. The Department, in conjunction with the federal government, studied the need for flood control in the state's flood plain areas.

During Leader's administration, 394 flood control projects were either completed, begun, or designed. These projects were undertaken not only to control floods when they occurred, but also to develop Pennsylvania's streams for recreation, for use by residents and industry, and for better watershed management. These projects were also part of the public work acceleration projects in 1958.

STATE PARK SYSTEM

George Leader referred to the state parks as "the type of medicine we need to ease the pressures of today's living." Leader's conservationist beliefs were particularly evident in this program. He and Secretary Goddard began expanding the state park system; this action conserved more than the natural areas. In his speeches, the Governor explained that his administration was devoted to conservation of human resources and natural resources. In the park program, the two converged. Leader saw mental health, good schools, and programs for the handicapped and injured workers as conservation. He also saw recreation as the conservation of human resources, and believed that people needed recreation to develop their full potential. The conservation of soil, water, and other natural resources was directly related to the conservation of human resources as well. "People nowadays," Leader said, "have more leisure time; our modern society is also subjecting them to increasing stresses and strains in their everyday living. Recreation becomes therapy more and more." The state parks not only preserved the water and forests, but also preserved human beings.

Following Pinchot's philosophy, Governor Leader felt that state parks should serve all citizens, and especially ordinary people. The wealthy had access to recreation in the private sector, but the middle and low income groups relied on the public facilities for recreation. Unfortunately Pennsylvania's population was concentrated mostly in the south eastern and western parts of the state, while the parks were generally located in the north central region.

The parks were not located in remote areas by accident. In 1898, the Forest Commission began acquiring land for the state forests; a large portion of this land was burnt over, poor farm land, or land with encumbered tax debts. Much of it was located in the north central part of the state. For recreation, people naturally sought quiet brooks or scenic woodlands. Foresters in these parks built primitive facilities in the frequently visited areas to help prevent forest fires and to improve sanitation. In the 1930's, the Civil Conservation Corps accelerated the development of the state forest land for recreation. Its camps were located in the north central region, because of the availability of public land for the camps. This large workforce improved the state forests, some of which were later designated as state parks. Roads, trails, cabins, and picnic areas, as well as forest conservation projects were completed. By 1955, forty-four state parks had been constructed, most of them located in the sparsely populated areas of the state.

A survey in the mid-1950's showed that only 9% of the population of Philadelphia used the state parks in a six-month period, while 85% of the population of Warren used the state parks during that time. To Secretary Goddard the results were significant; accessibility was the key to utilization. On a Pennsylvania map, he drew circles of 25 miles radius around each state park. It was obvious that the state parks, established to provide recreational areas for the citizens of the state, were located far from the centers of population. He chose twenty-five miles because the state parks were predominately day-use areas and a twenty-five mile trip was a reasonable distance to travel for recreation. Governor Leader was impressed with the idea of making the state parks accessible to Pennsylvanians and Secretary Goddard informed him that water was the key to successful mass use of the state parks. Boating, fishing, and swimming —attracted more people than picnic areas did. The twenty-five mile radius circles revealed two problems in the development of parks near populated areas: the availability of water and land acquisition. The first was easier to solve than the second, for once land was obtained, a dam could provide a reservoir for water sports. However, land acquisition was costly.

Obtaining funds for land acquisition was a perennial problem, it was especially a problem when you try to develop a park program which proposes to build parks near populated areas rather than on public land in the sparsely populated mountains of the state. Following California's procedure Secretary Goddard suggested the use of monies collected from the gas and oil leases for recreation, flood control, and conservation. The Republicans sponsored a state park development bill, combining these three objectives; it received bi-partisan support and passed in December 1955. The leases generated about 5 million dollars a year, which, instead of being deposited in the general fund, was used to finance land acquisition for new state parks and to build dams providing flood control and water for the parks.

Land, especially near the more densely populated areas of the state was expensive. George Leader urged the purchase of land before the prices climbed to levels where it would not be economically feasible for the state to buy the land for parks. A ring of parks was planned and built around Philadelphia and Pittsburgh, financed largely with gas and oil lease money.

However, this fund could not finance all the parks in the Goddard plan. In subsequent years, during the Lawrence and Scranton administrations, Secretary Goddard could point to the increased usage of the state park system to justify further expansion. The Project 70 bond issue of 70 million dollars added to federal revenues derived from liquid fuel taxes on boating, and gas and oil leases provided the financial base to locate a state park within twenty-five miles of almost every Pennsylvanian's home. Only in the sparsely populated areas of the state were the parks not built that close together.

The department was responsible for forty-four parks, forty-one forest picnic areas, thirteen forest monuments, eight historical parks, and three commissioned parks. Presque Isle State Park in Erie was badly damaged by storms in 1955; Leader asked for and received funds for road repairs and beach rebuilding to prevent land erosion in that park. The development of two historical sites, Point Park in Pittsburgh and the Mall in Philadelphia, was continued during Leader's term in office. The first winter sport park, Denton Hill in Potter County, was finished in January of 1959. One million dollars was appropriated for improvements to the forty-four existing parks. Attendance at the state parks soared from eight million in 1955 to twenty million people in 1958. Secretary Goddard credits the success of the state park program, which in 1978 had nearly twice as many parks as it did in 1955 (1978 attendance had reached 39 million), to Governor Leader's decision to fund the program with the gas and oil lease revenues, even though he was having difficulties with the passage of his budget in the legislature.

The Fish and Game Commissions cooperated in the development of the state park system. Despite their common responsibility for natural resources, the commissions and the Department of Forest and Waters had seldom interacted in the past. During the Leader administration, these three executive bodies cooperated on a number of projects. The expansion of hunting in the state parks provided 10,000 additional acres for hunting. On several occasions the Fish Commission purchased and developed lakes around which the new state parks were built. Their cooperation both helped to cut costs and produced larger, more comprehensive recreational areas.

PINCHOT STATE PARK

When Secretary Goddard approached Governor Leader with plans for a park in the Governor's home county of York, the Governor was concerned that the park would be misinterpreted as a political favor. Secretary Goddard assured him that it would not, because 179 municipalities had been investigated but only thirteen had been approved for state parks and the damming of Beaver Creek was a flood control project. Leader and his brother, Henry, suggested that the park be named for Governor Pinchot since Pinchot's first farm-to-market road was located next to the proposed site.

In 1958, George Leader broke ground for the new park. He noted how appropriate it was to name the park in memory of such a great conservationist. A few months later, Leader affirmed at a park dedication that "all we've tried to do is live up to Pinchot's standards."

The state park system, developed under Secretary Goddard, was primarily a year-round day-use, program, with camping rather than lodge facilities for overnight use. Two types of park areas were built: high-use areas and natural areas. They were sometimes located in the same park, other times in separate parks. The high-use Moraine Park and the natural park at McConnell's Mills in Western Pennsylvania are examples of the compromise between the naturalists' desire for wilderness and the business and sporting interests' desire for development. Secretary Goddard believed in moderation, or "use without abuse," as he termed his philosophy.

STATE FORESTS

When Secretary Goddard took office, he discovered a logging operation in Cook Forest State Park, located at the edge of the Allegheny National Forest. Goddard could not understand why there was logging in the park when there was available forest land in the proximity, so he placed an immediate stop to it. He also terminated a contract for logging on state land that had been granted in 1945. The company began logging in 1954 before the end of the previous administration, but permission was granted according to the terms of the 1945 contract. Goddard terminated the contract, calling it a questionable legal maneuver. He claimed to have saved the state $32,000 by cancelling the contract because of the increased price of lumber.

As there was controversy over the park program, there was controversy over forestry practices. There were those who believed that the state land should not be logged and others who believed that it is foolish to leave such a valuable resource untapped. Scientific timber management, begun by the previous administration, was continued and intensified under the direction of Secretary Goddard. Management plans for all the state forest lands were initiated; today, all state forests are closely managed.

There were reasons for logging the state forest other than the economics of wood production. Variation in the forest cover is important. Some desirable species of trees, such as ash, tulip poplar, and black cherry, do not grow well in shade. Game abounds in forests where the cover is a mixture of dense undergrowth and open areas. Clear-cutting, the practice of cutting all the trees in a forest, was a particularly strong point of disagreement. Secretary Goddard believed that controlled clear-cutting enhanced the state forest lands by varying it, developing different species, and different ages of trees, and providing good game habitats. He emphasized that clear-cutting had to be done scientifically in contours, and not extensively. Control was necessary to prevent soil erosion and maintain watersheds.

Most of the state's forests were managed under the concept of sustained yield, i.e., the production of the greatest possible sustained supply of timber, by reducing damage from fire, insects, and disease. In addition, the managed forests promoted recreation, protected watersheds, and provided a uniform supply of food and shelter for wild life. Sustained yield meant that lumber is harvested on a selective cutting basis that allows for maximum forest growth. If a forest acre was capable of producing a given number of board feet of lumber, then cutting less meant that the forest was not producing enough lumber and not developing properly because of overcrowding. However, if more than this number of board feet was taken, continued cutting would eventually eliminate the forest. Storms, fires, and other natural conditions also varied the yield of any given acre of forest. During the Leader administration, forests were under-cut, because they had been over-cut in the past. This practice allowed the forests to return to their maximum growth. Many industries and jobs depended on Pennsylvania timber products, and proper management meant preservation of those jobs.

A program of cooperative management similar to the agricultural extension program, was broadened during the Leader years. It offered small private timber owners, often farmers, professional advise on how to manage their woodlands. Department foresters recommended species of trees to plant, which trees to cut, and ways to get the best price for their lumber.

The department grew sixteen million seedlings, two-thirds of which were used to reforest strip mines. The state nurseries worked in conjunction with the Department of Mines and Mineral Industries, which was responsible for the reforestation of the scarred land.

Former department Secretary Lewis had ordered seedlings plowed under, because he claimed that they were unnecessary. This act particularly infuriated George Leader as an offense against nature and good husbandry. During his campaign, he had flown over vast sections of Pennsylvania scarred by strip mines and abandoned by the coal operators. Such scenes conjured up in the mind the all-too-common American practice of use-and-move-on. Leader felt that the plowed-under seedlings symbolized the wasted opportunities to recover and reclaim the scarred coal areas of the state.

Secretary Goddard's long term as a cabinet member compliments his theoretical concepts as a forester. The forester does not deal with daily production, as do many businessmen, or with yearly production, as do farmers. The forester thinks in long-range production. Eighty year plans, rather than yearly plans, are often required, because a forest grows slowly. Similarly, flood control projects and recreational facilities are not developed quickly. It is a credit to the governors who succeeded Leader to have kept Goddard on to complete part of his long-range plans in recreation, flood protection, and the conservation of natural resources.

GAME COMMISSION

The Pennsylvania Game Commission consisted of eight members who served without pay for eight-year terms. Like the members of the Fish Commission, they were knowledgeable in conservation and wildlife management. In 1952, the Commission elected Dr. Logan J. Bennett as its Executive Director. Dr. Bennett was a biologist and the author of several books on wildlife management, as well as an authority on training game dogs.

When Dr. Bennett died in 1957, the deputy director, Merton Golden, became acting Executive Director. He had worked for the Commission in various positions since 1920. Golden was elected as Executive Director in 1958 and served until 1965. The Executive Director, as Chief Game Warden of the Commission, supervised more than 270 employees charged with the protection and conservation of the state's wildlife, especially furbearing animals, fowl, and waterfowl.

The Commission was also responsible for hunting regulations. Hunting safety, conservation, and wildlife management were programs financed from hunting license fees. During Leader's administration, publicity campaigns informed the public of game management principles and the proper management of shelter and food supplies. The main misunderstanding seemed to concern the harvesting of the deer population. Some opposed doe hunting because it reduced the size of the herd that could be hunted. Others claimed that the herd was naturally regulated by food supply, and that without a controlled doe season, many deer would die of starvation during the winter. The argument has not yet been resolved.

During Leader's administration, the Game Commission and the Department of Forest and Waters allowed limited hunting in several state parks. The Game Commission purchased an additional 25,000 acres for state game lands for a total of 923,000 acres. The Leader years were ones of constructive concern for development and conservation of natural resources, wildlife preservation, and recreational opportunities.

FISH COMMISSION

The Pennsylvania Fish Commission was composed of eight persons, appointed without compensation for staggered eight-year terms. The Commissioners were persons who were knowledgeable and interested in conservation or fishing. In 1950, William Voigt was selected Executive Director by the Commission and continued to serve during the Leader administration. Voigt was an outstanding writer on the outdoors, and particularly on fishing. The Executive Director, as Chief Fish Warden, supervised more than 130 employees whose duty was to regulate fishing in state waters, enforce the motor boat laws, and educate the public. The commission produced fish at its hatcheries and conducted research on fish development. Pennsylvania lakes, rivers, and streams were stocked with more than seven million fish per year. The Commission raised mainly trout, a popular game fish which was the mainstay of many sporting goods businesses in the state. Thousands of trout were released in Pennsylvania's streams and lakes each year. The revenue from fishing licenses financed the Commission's operation, as well as its stocking program. Unfortunately, the hatchery-bred trout could not survive in the streams, so they had to be restocked each year.

Under Leader's administration, the Fish Commission began to stock the streams with muskellunges, a fish which, unlike the trout, can adapt to natural streams and reproduce in the wild. The addition of this fine game fish gave a new dimension to fishing in Pennsylvania.

The Commission built or purchased a number of lakes; it increased the number of fishing streams by acquiring access points to those streams. In cooperation with the Department of Forest and Waters, the Commission built several lakes on land purchased for state parks, thus extending opportunities for both recreation and fishing.

DEPARTMENT OF AGRICULTURE

Historically, Pennsylvania, has been and even today, is a major agricultural state. In 1790, the center of cereal crop production lay squarely within Pennsylvania's borders. All over the state from the rich Pennsylvania Dutch farmlands in Lancaster County to the grape arbors in Erie County, Pennsylvania is dotted with farms, most of them family farms. In 1955, Pennsylvania had the largest rural population in the nation, (people living on farms or in towns less than 2,500).

Pennsylvania's agriculture has been both extensive and diverse. In 1955, the dairy industry accounted for bringing 35 percent of the state's total farm cash income; poultry, (chickens, turkeys, eggs, and other fowl) generated 28 percent, the second highest portion. Livestock production included cattle, hogs, sheep, goats, and horses. Orchards and vineyards produced many varieties of fruits. In 1955, Pennsylvania produced 60 percent of the nation's mushrooms and also the most cigar leaf tobacco in the nation. These diverse agricultural ventures sustained a large agri-business of food processing, distribution, and farm suppliers. Related to the large dairy industry, Pennsylvania had the largest ice cream production of any state in the nation.

The Department of Agriculture was established in 1895 to regulate agricultural products and assist farmers. Protecting citizens from inferior produce, contaminated foods, and sick animals and plants were its regulatory functions. Testing and treating animals, research, marketing programs, and technical assistance were among the department's auxiliary functions. Agriculture was one of the smallest of the executive departments with 400 employees.

SELECTION OF THE
SECRETARY OF AGRICULTURE

One of George Leader's campaign promises was to select a farmer as his Secretary of Agriculture. He fulfilled that promise with his second cabinet selection, Dr. William Henning, who was, at the time, chairman of the Department of Animal Husbandry at the College of Agriculture of Pennsylvania State University. Not only had Dr. Henning been a professor of agriculture for thirty-one years, but he was also a successful farmer, maintaining a fine herd of Black Angus cattle. He achieved national recognition from his membership and leadership in many agricultural associations.

Dr. Henning had known Guy Leader, the Governor's father, through their shared interest in pure-bred livestock. Henning had worked with the senior Leader, when the latter was a state Senator, for legislation to improve the production of quality livestock on the Pennsylvania State University Campus. The association of these two farmers continued over the years, and George Leader came to know Dr. Henning to be a competent administrator, teacher, and farmer – an ideal person for the position of Secretary of Agriculture.

The pre-inaugural study highlighted the importance of the position of chief deputy for the operation of the department, who could handle much of the administrative work of the department's operations. A good deputy freed the Secretary for cabinet level responsibilities rather than the routine administrative duties in the department. Dr. Henning, with the approval of the Governor, selected Lee Bull[2], a county agent of the Pennsylvania State Agricultural Extension program to serve as chief deputy. Lee Bull had been a student of

Dr. Henning at Penn State. He became a county agent, first for Clinton County and later for other counties as well.

Many considered Secretary Henning to have been one of the state's best Agriculture Secretaries. He retained that position in the Governor Lawrence administration. Secretary Henning traveled extensively throughout the state, speaking with the farmers on many occasions. Because of his long tenure at Penn State, many of the Pennsylvania farmers were his former students. Secretary Henning's knowledge of Pennsylvania agriculture and its problems enabled him to promote the passage of useful legislation assisting and protecting farmers.

Secretary Henning welcomed the civil service system advocated by Governor Leader. Even though the personnel of the department were in general competent, a pre-inaugural study by Dr. Ferguson showed that morale was low due to low salaries, and no job classifications. The political basis for employment again had produced a conservative and uninnovative department.

When the executive board civil service program was made available, Secretary Henning expeditiously placed all of the department's technical heads under the program and conducted various training sessions for field employees to acquaint them with departmental procedures and new advances in their areas of expertise.

Another project which Secretary Henning tackled was the department's inadequate facilities; he dramatized their inadequacy by inviting legislators to visit the department on hot summer days letting them experience the uncomfortable working conditions first hand. New buildings were soon authorized, and in the next administration, the department moved to modern facilities.

---

[2]Lee Bull became Secretary of Agriculture under the Republican Governors Scranton and Shafer, after having served as deputy secretary under Secretary Henning in the Leader and Lawrence administration.

BUREAU OF MARKETS

The administration hired a marketing expert, John Rainy, to develop a complete marketing program for Pennsylvania's agricultural products. George Leader used the Somerset County Maple Festival to illustrate what could be done to enhance the marketing of Pennsylvania's products.

In Somerset, lumbermen offered to buy tall maple trees on many farms which had been a source of satisfaction and small income for many farm families. Usually the farmer tapped the maple trees each spring and made maple syrup and sugar, which was peddled door to door at a low price. Several men began marketing their maple products by mail and, through improved marketing techniques, soon had a flourishing business.

The maple trees were saved from the lumbermen's axe and their syrup and sugar supplemented the farmer's income. Leader asked, "If the production of maple syrup and sugar can be so rejuvenated, why can't the same thing be done with potatoes or apples or any one of Pennsylvania's many farm products?" He was certain that similar marketing approaches could be successful for other products.

With the assistance of a federal grant of $10,000, the Bureau of Markets began a program to enhance Pennsylvania's marketing techniques. The Governor formed the Food Marketing Advisory Committee to develop ideas. This committee of farmers, food processors, distributors, and retailers suggested various programs which the bureau implemented to increase the sale of Pennsylvania products. One such program was the designation of special time periods to highlight particular products, such as Egg Month, Peach Week, Apple Week, and Mushroom Week. These special weeks and months, declared by the Governor, drew statewide attention to that product. Improved advertising and packaging were also encouraged. A volunteer egg certification program was established to improve the market quality of eggs; it was quickly adopted by most egg producers and resulted in increased egg sales.

OTHER BENEFITS FOR FARMERS

Pennsylvania farmers used large quantities of liquid fuel in production. Although much of the equipment powered by these fuels, such as conveyors and generators, had no wheels, the farmer paid 6¢ per gallon in tax for highway construction and maintenance. Since most farm equipment, even gasoline-powered wheeled vehicles, did not use the highways, it was illogical for farmers to subsidize highways at a higher percentage (because of their farm equipment) than the general public. The legislature had enacted a law to refund 50 percent of that liquid fuel tax to the farmers. During the Leader administration a temporary measure was passed to return the full tax amount. In 1957, this measure became permanent, and the farmer was relieved of $60 in taxes per 1,000 gallons of liquid fuel. The Governor considered the refund one of his administration's most important achievements in the area of agriculture.

Another law welcomed by the farmers was the provision which removed the restrictions on fishing in a farmer's own pond. This legislation enabled the farmer and his family to fish without licenses or limits in their own pond providing it was not fed from a stocked stream.

Under the direction of Secretary Henning, conservation became an integral part of the department's program. With pride, Henning wrote in his final report to Governor Leader that twenty county-wide soil conservation districts were established in the four years while only thirty had been created in the previous ten years. Nine watershed flood prevention projects were established and a soil testing program was instituted in conjunction with Penn State and the Soil Conservation Service.

Leader's views of the role of agriculture were historical and basic. He deeply respected Pennsylvania's agricultural heritage and knew the historical significance of the independent farm in the development of the republic. He was born into an industrial and technological America that would have confounded Jefferson, but he was Jeffersonian in his conviction that the farming community was important as a producer of food and commodities, but also as a seed-bed of character, independence, and self-reliance. Though not a sentimentalist; Leader's support for the preservation of the rural community is deeply rooted in personal experience.

MILK CONTROL COMMISSION

State control of milk production began in Pennsylvania in 1934. A Commission of three members, appointed by the Governor with Senate approval, is responsible for the supervision and regulation of the milk industry. The Commission licenses milk dealers but more importantly it fixes the prices which dealers pay milk producers and the prices which the dealers can charge the consumers. The Commission had 73 employees working in three divisions.

George Leader appointed two new members to the Commission, but their confirmation was delayed in the Senate until the middle of 1956. The Republican Senators did not cooperate with Leader on a number of appointments, because they were convinced that Leader's victory was an accident in Pennsylvania politics and that the Republicans would regain power in the next election. These Republicans had grown accustomed to having the power in Pennsylvania and now they exerted it visibly, in a way to show Leader who was still boss, by holding up his appointments. This crass political behavior also kept a number of Republicans in jobs because the old appointees remained in office until new appointees were approved by the Senate.

Leader reappointed Joab K. Mahood, the Chairman of the Commission, appointed in 1952 by Governor Fine. Mahood was a farmer from northwest Pennsylvania who was active in state farm organizations. John A. Smith, a Democrat, was appointed by Leader in 1956. Smith, also a farmer, had served two terms in the State House of Representatives. Simon K. Uhl, a lawyer from Somerset County, was also appointed in 1956.

Leader, being a farmer and familiar with rural life, was very sensitive to the problems of the farmers in general and in particular to the problems faced by the dairy farmers. Although the Governor had no direct control over the actions of the Milk Control Commission, he could encourage the Commission to deal with certain issues. In May 1955, Leader wrote to the Commission and suggested changes in the milk control regulation. Subsequent hearings convinced the Commission to adopt changes in the regulations to allow lower prices for milk sold in half-gallon containers.

The sixty-three state institutions purchased milk at fixed prices, through favored contracts with no requirements for quality. Leader's milk plan proposed to allow state institutions to purchase milk at wholesale prices, because of the large volume of sales. Federal institutions in Pennsylvania did not purchase milk at fixed retail prices; and a study showed that milk sold to those institutions was 5¢ a gallon cheaper than that sold to the state institutions. Leader contended that the state could save a substantial amount each year if it purchased milk at the wholesale price. A discount plan was implemented and competitive bidding replaced favored contracts.

In some areas milk produced on Pennsylvania farms was sold out of state and, therefore, the price was not controlled by Pennsylvania regulations. Federal regulations applied in some instances but in a number of areas neither federal nor state regulations controlled milk prices. Dairy farmers were selling their milk to dealers in New York and New Jersey below the usual price that other farmers were getting for their milk. These dealers, by transporting milk across state lines, were purchasing milk cheaper but not passing the savings on to the consumers; thus making large profits at the expense of the Pennsylvania farmers. Leader established a fourteen member committee to study the problem and as a result of the work of the committee, federal regulations established price controls on milk produced in northeast Pennsylvania. This new regulation meant a 10% increase for some 1800 dairy farmers in the northeast.

One of the problems facing dairy farmers and the Milk Control Commission was the determination of the cost of milk production. During the Leader administration, the Commission, in cooperation with Pennsylvania State University, developed a cost questionnaire that was distributed to dairy farmers throughout the state. This sophisticated cost accounting analysis helped farmers to assess more objectively the cost of milk production.

Leader was not an advocate of inflated milk prices to give the farmer advantageous prices, rather he was interested in a fair price and increased milk consumption to help the dairy farmers. By increasing consumption, Leader sought to increase farm income, lower the federal subsidy to the farmers (which was one-half the regular price of milk), and improve public health.

The administration actively supported promotional activities to increase milk consumption. Encouraging school children to drink more milk through school lunch programs, coupled with the allowance of chocolate milk for school lunches, resulted in the doubling of milk consumption by school children. The administration also established a dairy bar in the State Capitol and initiated the use of milk vending machines in the state office buildings and institutions. Leader personally encouraged private industry to install milk vending machines in their plants and places of business. Leader pointed out that agriculture and industry worked hand-in-hand by making milk accessible to persons who normally did not have it available. Industry helped the dairy farmer who in turn would purchase more products from industry.

DEPARTMENT OF MINES AND MINERAL INDUSTRIES

Coal, the backbone of Pennsylvania's industrial strength in the 1800's, was being replaced by gas and oil in the mid-1900's. Coal production had dropped from 213 million tons in the 1920's to 99 million tons in 1954. Diesel engines had replaced the coal-powered locomotives, and natural gas was replacing coal furnaces in Pennsylvania homes. Coal had not only been the backbone of Pennsylvania's industry, but also was the mainstay of many Pennsylvania communities. Small mining towns dotted the state, and with the decline in coal production these communities became pockets of long term unemployment. The Leader administration approached this problem through the Department of Commerce's economic development program. The decline in the production of coal did not automatically end the coal industry, since coal remained a basic necessity for the making of steel, and the increased demand for electric power in the state offset some of the loss of market for coal in other areas. In 1955, about 100,000 coal miners still worked in 3,500 coal mines in the state.

Pennsylvania's coal deposits lie in two general regions: the anthracite region in the northeast, and the bituminous region in the west. Anthracite coal is older, harder coal and more desirable of the two because it burns cleaner. Both types of coal are extracted either from beneath the earth through deep mines, or from open pits near surface level after the overburden is removed.

Mining is a hazardous enterprise both above and below the ground; poisonous gas, cave-ins, and explosions are constant perils for miners. Mine subsidence, underground fires, and flooded mines cause problems for the general public years after the coal has been removed and the mine abandoned. Because of these hazards and the press to protect our natural resources, the state enacted legislation aimed at controlling the coal mining industry. The Department of Mines, established in 1903, replaced the Bureau of Mines of the Department of Internal Affairs; it was responsible for the enforcement of mining regulations. As laws and regulations tightened over the years, the safety record of the Pennsylvania mines improved. In 1907, there were 514 mine-related deaths; in 1950 there was only one-tenth as many fatalities, a dramatic decrease even in view of reduced mining activity. The dramatic reduction in the number of deaths and a corresponding decline in injuries was attributed to stricter legislation and union pressures. Subsequent major disasters give proof that neither legislation nor union power had taken the deadly peril out of mining.

SELECTION OF THE SECRETARY OF MINES

The vigor of enforcement of mining laws depended primarily on the direction given by the administration. A Secretary of Mines chosen from the ranks of coal mine operators might not have been as strict in enforcing regulations. A Secretary chosen from the ranks of the miners would probably identify more closely with the miners' concern for safety. George Leader selected a miner for his Secretary of Mines. Joseph Kennedy, a leader in the United Mine Workers, had worked in the mines for a number of years before being employed by the union. He became secretary to the President of District #1 in 1929 and was the administrative assistant to the vice-president of the United Mine Workers at the time George Leader invited him to direct the Department of Mines.

As in other departments, reorganization was the first priority in the Department of Mines. The two field offices became divisions of the department, giving the deputy secretaries in charge of these offices more autonomy and authority to enforce mining regulations.

Lewis Evans was named deputy secretary for the bituminous region. His office in Ebensburg was responsible for 2,172 mines and 69,000 miners. To perform its function, the office had one roof inspector, two electrical inspectors, six strip mine inspectors, and thirty deep mine inspectors. Daniel Connelly, deputy secretary for the anthracite region, had an office in Wilkes-Barre with one roof inspector, one electrical inspector, three strip mine inspectors, and twenty-five deep mine inspectors. Both deputy secretaries had had extensive experience as working miners and mine inspectors.

The Legislature created a new Division of Oil and Gas in this reorganization. The division was responsible for the enforcement of recent legislation that prescribed regulations for underground storage of oil and gas and controlled the relationship between that storage and nearby coal operations. W. Roy Cunningham directed the division; he had six oil and gas inspectors in the field. The name of the Department of Mines was changed to Mines and Mineral Industries. The Leader administration also intended to move the Division of Mine Quarries and Explosives from the Department of

Labor and Industry to the Department of Mines and Mineral Industries. This division was responsible for safety inspection of limestone, sandstone, clay, and oil mines, quarries, and plants where explosives were manufactured. Various studies of state government recommended consolidating the inspection of all mining operations; however, the administration was unable to effect the merger.

The pre-inaugural study written by G. R. Fitterer, Dean of the School of Engineering and Mines at the University of Pittsburgh, described general mining laws and the recent improvements in these laws passed during the Fine administration. Among the study's constructive suggestions were those which would increase the department's involvement in the pressing problems of mine sealing and strip mine reclamation.

MINE SAFETY

One of the department's principle obligations was mine safety, a responsibility of critical importance to the miners and their families. Mining is certainly one of the most hazardous occupations. George Leader was proud that safety records continued to improve during the years of his administration. A great deal of this progress is attributable to improvements in roof safety initiated during the Fine administration. Since most of the deep mine disasters were the result of roof cave-ins the Department of Mines began to require the bolting of mine roofs to make them more secure. The safety of miners was further assured when the administration obtained a law requiring the inspection of all mines. Previously, bituminous mines employing five or fewer miners were exempted from safety inspections.

Contrary to common expectation, patronage did not control the selection of mine inspectors. They were appointed by the Governor from a list of qualified applicants. To qualify, an individual must have had five years experience working in the mines and have passed an examination. Requiring experience helped to ensure a positive attitude toward mine safety. Safety inspection was considered so important that every mine was inspected twice a year by state inspectors and annually by federal mine inspectors. This check system of state and federal inspection minimized the likelihood that safety violations would be overlooked or ignored.

Despite these precautions, mining accidents still occurred. To assist in the event of such disasters, the department maintained mine rescue units in Uniontown, Johnstown, and Girardville. Each unit had two men trained in mine rescue and well equipped vehicles prepared for emergencies. In addition to being on the alert for mining accidents, these men conducted educational programs for miners on mine rescue and first aid.

STRIP MINES

Conservation of natural resources was a recurrent theme in Leader's administration. As in the Departments of Forest and Waters and Agriculture, the Department of Mines and Mineral Industries' personnel adhered to the principle of *use not abuse*. This approach governed the administration's strip mining policies. The elimination of strip mines would have denied the state and its citizens of a tremendous part of their livelihood. Yet to allow coal operators to mine indiscriminately would have been equally disasterous. Already the land was badly scarred. Employees who traveled with the Governor by air relate that he was horrified to observe the extent of the devastation to the state caused by open pit and strip mining.

Prior to the passage of new strip mine reclamation legislation in 1953, the Department of Mines was responsible for backfilling strip mines, and the Department of Forest and Waters was responsible for the restoring of backfilled land. This division of responsibility was ineffective. Under Leader, the Department of Mines became solely responsible for the entire reclamation program. Between 1955 and 1956, 21,000 acres were restored and planted as compared to 24,000 acres in the entire decade from 1945 to 1954. George Leader further proposed the conversion of reclaimed strip mines to lakes for recreation and conservation.

Strip mining abuses were flagrant and common. Intensive lobbying by the coal industry had much to do with their continuation. Prior legislation was not always strong enough to force coal operators to backfill their mines; even when the law was adequate, the enforcement of the regulations was often delinquent. Strip mine inspectors, unlike deep mine inspectors, were patronage employees until Leader's administration; thus, politics often won out over proper land reclamation.

Mine operators exploited loopholes in the laws ingeniously. For instance, they would extract 90 percent of the coal from a mine, leave a piece of old equipment at the site and move to another mine. When ordered to backfill the mine, they would point out that the mine was still active; thus the owners evaded the expense of backfilling. Another common practice was for operators to carry one bond for a number of mines. The law required every strip mine operator to post a bond of $300 per acre of land to be mined. This bond would be forfeited if the mine was not backfilled and planted. The money covered the department's expenses for backfilling the site. Coal operators often obtained one bond and showed it for several mines. Their tactic would not be discovered in time, and the department would not have sufficient funds for reclamation. Through the use of civil service strip mine inspectors and the mapping of all mining operations in the state, the Department of Mines and Mineral Industries began to correct these abuses.

DEEP MINES

Abandoned mines caused mine subsidence, underground fires, and mine flooding. The old Department of Mines had merely sealed the abandoned mines, based on the assumption that the acid water would eventually turn alkaline. Research and experience clearly demonstrated that sealing the mine was not adequate alone, because the mines had to be drained to remove the acid water. To eliminate underground fires and mine subsidence, the mines had to be filled as well.

The 1953 mining law authorized the Department of Mines to seal, dewater, and extinguish fires. The department engaged private contractors to flush the deep mines. This process involved drilling six inch holes into the mines from the surface. A mixture of earth and water was dumped into the holes to fill the mine. Previously, only five different contractors sealed abandoned mines. One of Governor Leader's first official acts was to stop all contract work not awarded by competitive bidding. With competitive bidding, twenty-eight contractors were awarded mine sealing contracts during Leader's administration. With federal matching funds a program of anthracite mine drainage began; this drainage was necessary to prevent the flooding of the anthracite formations.

Early in the administration, the Commonwealth Disaster Committee was called to Natalie, a small town in central Pennsylvania, to inspect a mine fire that had been burning for three months and was spewing obnoxious fumes over the town. Although this incident was not a disaster, because the fumes were not dangerous, it alerted Leader to the need for an effective waste disposal law. The practice of using abandoned strip mines as dump sites was common around the state. Landfills could have been an acceptable way of utilizing those open pits abandoned before the 1953 reclamation legislation. The major disadvantage lay in the prevalence of dumpfires either accidentally or intentionally started. When fires in the garbage dump ignited coal seams, a more dangerous situation arose that led to vast inconvenience, property destruction, and a significant waste of coal. The new law required the acquisition of permits issued by the Department of Mines and Mineral Industries before any dumping could occur.

George Leader was concerned about the pockets of labor surplus, and he tried to conquer the state's high unemployment rate with his job development program in the Department of Commerce. He went a step further in the coal communities, besides trying to attract new industry into these areas and retrain the workers for new jobs, Leader established the Coal Research Board to identify new uses and markets for Pennsylvania coal. This seven member board sponsored twenty-two coal research projects to investigate ways to save the declining coal production and save the jobs that were being lost to automation.

Legislation, in the Fine administration, had laid ground-work for improvements in the mining industry. Leader used his managerial expertise to effect important reorganization. He fought against patronage, corruption, and economic favoritism toward vested interests. Consistently here, as elsewhere, the statesman is seen in his concern for people, for conservation, for efficient management.

Planning a new look for Pittsburgh.

Chapter 5

Commerce And Public Services

DEPARTMENT OF COMMERCE

The Department of Commerce had been established by the Republicans during the James administration, in 1939, to promote commerce, business, and industry in the state. In Leader's view, the department had degenerated into a "third-rate publicity operation," that primarily catered to Republican political and business interests. Pennsylvania Democrats were full of criticism, but divided as to the problem and its solution. Commerce departments generally extoll the virtues of "free enterprise" and advertise the hazards of extensive governmental regulation and control. They can frequently be the mouthpiece of development and construction lobbies, as their function is to induce industry to locate in their state. Favors such as tax advantages, a guaranteed supply of cheap labor, and pro-business legislation are often offered as inducements.

The author of the Chesterman Report (1953) recommended the abolition of the department because of its expenditure of public money for mere promotional activities. Two of the department's most blatantly political aspects were its clipping service and its operation of Pennsylvania Week. The clipping service, the assembly of articles discussing administration programs and policies in newspapers throughout the state, was, in effect, a means of polling public opinion statewide on the operation of the administration. The political nature of Pennsylvania Week was more obvious; this week promoting the Commonwealth was a convenient way for Republicans to get good political exposure, at the state's expense, just prior to elections.

SELECTION OF THE
SECRETARY OF COMMERCE

During his campaign, George Leader promised to make the Department of Commerce a vital part of state government. His pledge to stop Pennsylvania Week symbolized his goal of removing politics from the department and making economic development its primary function. To accomplish these objectives, Leader sought a Secretary of Commerce with expertise in economic development. He first offered the position to William Batt, who declined. Jack Robin, who had been executive secretary to the Mayor of Pittsburgh, was then approached. Robin was involved with Pittsburgh's economic development program and was a logical choice since he had helped formulate the economic policies for Leader's campaign. Robin also wrote the controversial inaugural speech in which Leader accused Governor Fine and the Republican Party of destroying the state's financial position. The speech surprised Governor Fine who expected to be complimented for extending full cooperation to the Leader transition team, the customary political gesture. Leader was not one to contradict his campaign promises and beliefs for political etiquette. Leader repeatedly shocked the politicians of both camps by his lack of interest in conventional political game-playing.

Secretary Robin did what George Leader hoped he would. He eliminated the clipping service, Pennsylvania Week, and the travel bureau. Many department employees were dismissed. His actions were deemed excessively drastic by other cabinet officers who had been instructed by the Governor to retain qualified personnel. Robin did not believe that most of the department's employees were qualified to achieve the department's new mandate to initiate an economic development program for the state.

Robin's actions ruffled a few feathers, especially when he cancelled the newspaper subscriptions sent to the clipping service. He was justifiably embarrassed to find that his requests for the return of the unused portion of the subscription fees were answered by irritated publishers who informed the Secretary that the papers were sent free of charge to the state.

George Leader experienced firsthand some consequences of the swiftness of Robin's actions. One day a young woman came into the Governor's Office to take his picture for official publications. A few days later a fine picture reached the Governor. On seeking the young woman out for congratulations, he learned that she had just been fired as part of Secretary Robin's reorganization.

In addition to reorganizing the Department of Commerce, Robin began the industrial development program by hiring experienced economists and assembling the economic development package which Leader presented to the General Assembly in March 1955. This plan included the creation of the Coal Research Board and development programs for industry, natural resources, highways, and urban areas. The Governor concurrently requested the legislature to solicit more federal assistance so that Pennsylvania would have its fair share from federal revenue.

Jack Robin resigned in September 1955 to join the Regional Industrial Development Corporation in Pittsburgh. George Leader again offered the position of Secretary of Commerce to Bill Batt, who again declined. Robin recommended William Davlin, a professional he had recruited to head up the Bureau of Industrial Development. Davlin was an economist and a graduate of the University of Wisconsin. Before coming to Pennsylvania, he had served as a consultant on industrial and market development to the U.S. Department of Commerce, Delta Airlines, and the State of Kentucky.

Robin remained active in state government as chairman of the State Planning Board. This fifteen member board was created by the first Reorganization Plan of 1955. The state's overall planning was transferred from the Department of Commerce to the Board which reported directly to the Governor. This change freed the Planning Board from departmental control, made it bi-partisan, and removed the routine administrative tasks of coordinating local planning efforts. The Board was thus able to study larger and broader concerns, such as the effects of atomic energy development and the St. Lawrence Seaway on Pennsylvania. It also studied the economic consequences of the decline in coal and iron ore production and reviewed the development and control of the state's larger river basins.

INDUSTRIAL DEVELOPMENT

State government programs are circular, each tied directly or indirectly to others. George Leader recognized this relationship and spoke of its importance. Welfare and education programs and workmens' benefits required tax revenue for their operation. In Pennsylvania, these revenues came mainly from corporate and sales taxes; thus, strong industries and businesses were necessary to generate sufficient funds. Without these funds, there would be no programs for the needy. Pennsylvania had 319,000 persons unemployed in 1955. Four of the nation's nine areas with labor surplusses in excess of 12 percent were located in the state. In many parts of the state, the unemployment rate was at least 6 percent. The unemployed took from the general fund but obviously did not contribute to it. Leader wanted full employment, because it meant productive people, rather than lost talent, increased revenues rather than depleted funds, and more money, therefore, for social programs.

Leader urged the public not to think of the unemployed as statistics. "They are not just statistics," he asserted, "each one of these cold figures represents an able-bodied man or woman who wants to work and cannot find a job; every one represents a family who cannot maintain a decent living standard on a substandard income; each one represents a person in distress."

In many areas of the state, there was only a single industry: steel, coal, lumber, textiles, railroads. As the market for coal shrank and automation spread, many jobs were lost. The state produced more steel but employed the same number of workers. As diesel engines replaced the coal burners, railroad maintenance jobs decreased. Textile firms moved south to take advantage of cheaper labor; towns were left without industry when lumber companies moved away from "cut out" areas. Leader stressed that "no magic formula will ever exist for economic transformation, for an overnight change to diversity rather than uniformity in industrial production and employment." However, he did not let this discourage his administration's efforts to end unemployment.

The main objectives of the newly reorganized Department of Commerce were to foster economic development in low employment areas and to increase Pennsylvania's share of the nation's business and industrial growth. Like other states, Pennsylvania tried to attract new industry, however, it was no longer the most desirable state for development because of cheaper labor elsewhere and the abundance of gas and oil in the southwest.

The administration's first industrial development bill did not pass through the legislature. This proposal sought $20,000,000 for an Industrial Development Authority that would build factories to lease or sell to companies willing to locate in Pennsylvania. Discouraged by the lack of support for the bill, Governor Leader held public hearings on the industrial development program. He and Secretaries Davlin and Torquato traveled to Wilkes-Barre, Erie, Altoona, and Johnstown to discuss local industrial development programs and hear suggestions for amending the administration's industrial development legislation.

Industrial development was not a new concept in Pennsylvania or around the nation. Among the first industrial developers were the railroad companies and the electric utilities. These companies tried to attract industries into their service areas so that they could move more freight and sell more power. Industrial realtors were the next type of industrial developers to enter the scene. Such promoters tried to attract new industry into buildings and facilities which had been left vacant by other industries.

When the anthracite coal industry in the Northeast of Pennsylvania declined, thousands were left unemployed and the region was economically depressed. A bootstrap operation was begun in Scranton to collect money for the construction of buildings to be leased or sold to companies that located in the area. It was a total community effort; banks and insurance companies put up about 65 percent of the mortgage money. The money from leases and sales and from the equity of the buildings provided the capital for new industrial facilities. By 1955, fifty-five new plants had been built in Scranton and sixty-five businesses had expanded in ten years. Despite these efforts, the area still had a high level of unemployment. The Scranton Plan was by no means a cosmetic gesture, but the underlying economic distress was greater than what purely local effort could change.

The bootstrap ideas spread to other communities in Pennsylvania. The local achievements throughout the state were very impressive. Between the end of the Second World War and 1955, eighty communities had built 112 factories, employing an estimated 26,600 persons. In the public hearings, Leader found two points on which the people unanimously agreed: there was not enough money to continue building, because their money was tied up in past projects, and they wanted the state's assistance. The administration developed a new industrial development proposal which passed in May 1956. The act authorized the establishment of the Pennsylvania Industrial Development Authority (PIDA) and appropriated five million dollars for loans to local industrial development agencies. An additional million dollars was added in the 1957 session.

The state could not legally lend money to private enterprises; it could, however, build and lease buildings, as the first plan proposed, or lend money to local development agencies. The authority was authorized to lend up to 30 percent of the total construction costs to local agencies in communities with a 6 percent unemployment rate for three years and to communities with an unemployment rate of 9 percent for a minimum of eighteen months. The local agencies had to supply 20 percent of the cost and the industry was required to obtain the first mortgage through conventional means. This arrangement accomplished several objectives. It gave more funds to the local industrial development agencies and relieved the state of the need to establish an elaborate bureaucracy to locate new industry. It tended to discourage undesirable and high risk operations by requiring companies to find coventional loans first. It required the local community to commit itself financially and guaranteed minimum local involvement and motivation. Finally, it provided lower interest rates overall. The combination of 50 percent loans at conventional rates and the 50 percent local and state loans at low interest rates produced an arrangement attractive to development.

The PIDA program was very successful. In its thirty months of operation during the Leader administration, the authority lent money for the construction or expansion of seventy-one buildings. This provided employment for 11,800 persons. In addition to the PIDA program, the legislature passed the Pennsylvania Industrial Assistance Act, which appropriated one million dollars for matching grants to local industrial development and Chambers of Commerce, for expenses incurred in research, promotion, or the operation of their organization. This bill helped to regain some of the good will lost in the business community by curtailment of promotional programs.

Pennsylvania relied heavily on corporate taxes for its revenues, but the taxes were not overburdening. The department had the responsibility to demonstrate that Pennsylvania's taxes were not very different from those in other states. Leader did, however, heed the advice of his committee and lifted the machinery tax in Allegheny County.

Because of traditional differences in political philosophies, the new Democratic governor was thought to be "anti-business," a suspicion which increased during the Westinghouse strike of 1955. At the advice of a fact-finding board, Leader declared the strike a lockout, thereby entitling the workers to unemployment compensation. This move led to a quick settlement of the strike. The PIDA program helped to dispel his anti-business image but as Leader always believed, the press in Pittsburgh was never convinced.

Governor Leader testified twice before a congressional committee on the Federal Area Redevelopment bill before Congress. He emphasized the achievements of the local communities and the success with which the now nationally recognized PIDA program furthered the efforts. However, Leader stressed that state actions alone could not result in full employment, especially in economically depressed areas. The federal bill, which would have provided assistance for both urban redevelopment was passed by Congress but vetoed by President Eisenhower. George Leader and four other governors sent letters and telegrams to convince the President not to veto a bill which they felt was needed to combat unemployment. When the President vetoed the bill, Governor Leader expressed his regret that the President did not meet with the governors and listen to their opinions on the need for the area redevelopment bill. Leader believed that the bill was vetoed because the President received poor advice about the workability of the rural redevelopment section. Leader knew that the bill was not perfect, but it was a step in the right direction. Moreover, he had proof in Pennsylvania that rural redevelopment was a workable solution to area unemployment.[1]

Even before Leader initiated his industrial development program, several industries had moved to Pennsylvania. The biggest disappointment, however, was the much publicized Curtis-Wright venture, a project to establish an aeronautical and rocket testing facility in Clearfield and Elk Counties. A large tract of state land was leased to the company, and more land was sold outright and developed by the company. This project would have meant the creation of many jobs and the overall development of that area. Unfortunately, the federal government changed its plans about sponsoring such technology, and the project was dropped. The state regained title to the land, but disappointment lingered for some time.

TRAVEL BUREAU

Since Secretary Robin had abolished the travel bureau, there was a void in the state's services to the tourist trade. Pennsylvania had several tourist and recreational areas which badly needed promotional assistance. George Leader had called the Department of Commerce a third-rate promotion agency and did not intend to tolerate any substandard operation in his administration. Tourism was, however, the seventh largest industry in the state, providing one billion dollars gross intake annually. Bill Davlin wanted to reinstate the Travel Bureau to promote the state's rich and varied tourist attractions and the fine hunting and fishing opportunities that the mountains and farm lands provided. He sought to enhance Pennsylvania's deserved share of America's tourism, recreation, and vacation trade.

Davlin asked Harold Swenson, Executive Director of the Pocono Mountain Vacation Bureau, to prepare a plan for the

---

[1]The Redevelopment Bill was passed under President Kennedy, who appointed Bill Batt to serve as the director of the redevelopment program.

projected tourist bureau. Because the plan was well received, Secretary Davlin searched for someone to head up the new bureau. His search seemed fruitless, until someone suggested that the director of tourism for the Poconos was surely qualified, and that was, of course, none other than Harold Swenson, the author of the plan. Swenson was both very active in the tourist trade and was serving as the executive secretary of the Stroudsburg Chamber of Commerce. By interest and by temperament, Swenson was ready to undertake his job with great enthusiasm. He labelled the atmosphere of the administration, "ecstatic," for it was young and energetic. If they did not have all the right answers, at least they had the energy to seek them in action.

Swenson tried to instill a new spirit in the state's travel and tourist industry. He wanted Pennsylvania's recreational areas to enhance the economic development program, thereby adding another dimension to the bureau's importance. Pennsylvania could lure companies with extensive hunting, fishing, camping, and travel opportunities stressing their potential use by their employees. Although the bureau concentrated on statewide advertising, it also assisted the development of local tourist areas. One such area was the Pennsylvania-Dutch tourist area in Lancaster County.

DEPARTMENT OF HIGHWAYS

In addition to conservation programs, Governor Pinchot is also remembered for "taking the farmer out of the mud" by increasing and improving the state's highway system. As a result of his efforts, Pennsylvania's state highway system in 1955 extended for more miles than the highways in all of the New England states, New York, and New Jersey combined. The Department of Highways replaced the Commissioner of Highways, first appointed in 1903. The Department of Highways was formed in 1925 to manage the increasing number of state highways. By 1955, there were more than 41,000 miles of state highways, a figure which did not include the roads under local jurisdiction.

The Department of Highways was one of the most political departments in the state government. It was the largest department, and only one-third of the 14,500 employees had technical or professional expertise. Most were laborers and unskilled workers. The department's eleven highway districts were divided along county lines, and the country chairmen exerted considerable influence over the hiring practices for both professional and unskilled positions. Most work at the district level involved maintenance and construction; laboring jobs were among those most easily filled by patronage. However, the professional positions were also filled by patronage; and this practice deterred many capable engineers from seeking work with the state.

Undesirable political influence extended still further. The establishment of priorities for road and bridge construction was often determined by politics rather than by need. Democrats accused Republicans in the Fine administration of "forced work" in the months before the 1954 election. The Democrats claimed that the Republicans transferred money into predominately Democratic counties to improve the roads, trying to attract votes for Republican candidates. Another way of showing political favor was the placement of local roads under the state highway system, thereby freeing local governments from maintenance costs; in each session an omnibus bill was passed to incorporate more local roads into the state system.

The pre-inaugural study conducted by Henry Harral emphasized the need for recruiting competent professionals for technical positions. Low salaries and poor job security, both due to the political nature of the department, exacerbated the problem. This study also highlighted the lack of planning as a major weakness in the department. Harral found that the chief engineer carried a small notepad in which he noted highway needs throughout the state. This constituted his planning document. Other studies of the department also emphasized the need for an adequate planning program to improve the state's highway system. Harral also recommended the creation of a chief deputy to free the Secretary from routine duties and provide for more involvement in cabinet level decisions.

SELECTION OF THE SECRETARY OF HIGHWAYS

George Leader wanted to find a post for his old friend and political ally, Joe Lawler. The Department of Highways was so political that Leader felt that a seasoned politician would be best able to run it. Lawler was, however, not just a political appointment. He was a competent administrator who had been a first assistant postmaster under President Truman. Leader was certain that if Lawler could manage the organization of a large bureaucracy like the postal system, where he had supervised a million employees, he could direct Pennsylvania's Department of Highways. However, Leader's primary reason for selecting Lawler was his integrity, a virtue attested to by everyone who knew him. With all the politics in the department, Leader wanted someone who would be beyond reproach, so he would not have to be concerned with scandals in the highway department.

Despite Lawler's integrity, the department unfortunately did not have a scandal-free record. In 1957, a cinder supplier bribed department employees in three counties to have them pay for cinders that were not delivered. The irregularity was discovered, and the employees involved were immediately dismissed. Leader reiterated his intention to fire anyone found guilty of wrong doing in his administration. Nevertheless, the public still associated the scandal with the administration, despite its efforts to remain honest.

The selection of the chief engineer was difficult. This person had to be a professional, and few engineers with the necessary qualifications wanted the position because salaries were significantly higher in private industry. Leader appointed General Richards, a retired army engineer, who served only a few months. Harral had suggested in the pre-inaugural study that a chief engineer might be selected from the district engineers. However, many of them left the department when the parties changed control because they feared that they would be fired or because they found better jobs elsewhere. It was reported that some were actually fired against the wishes of the new governor. Secretary Lawler found Art Wiesberger of Allentown to be both competent and willing to accept the post of chief engineer. He spent several months as a district engineer to familiarize himself with the operation of the department and district level problems. While he was district engineer in Eastern Pennsylvania, hurricanes Connie and Diana hit Pennsylvania. Wiesberger spent several weeks in the Poconos, assessing the damage to the roads, helping to evacuate children from the camps, and building temporary bridges. He became chief engineer in October of 1955 and effectively reorganized the department. Unfortunately, he had a heart attack which left him with doctor's orders to resign from the department because he had overworked himself. He was replaced by Robert Farley.

POLITICS OF HIGHWAY CONSTRUCTION

The Department of Highways was and remains a political battleground. Politics had influenced many personnel policies of the department in the past, and politics remained entrenched in the department under Leader. The Governor said that he gave his "pound of flesh" in the highway department in order to gain what he wanted in many other departments. Only here did Leader compromise with the party over the merit system. He was able to have only the technical and professional positions added to the executive board of civil service. Nearly 10,000 jobs in the Department of Highways remained under the patronage system.

A recurring political claim is that the party in power did not do enough highway construction and maintenance. The Republicans depicted Leader's Department of Highways as a poorly managed department that failed to improve Pennsylvania's highways. That assertion was countered by Joe Lawler, who criticized the political activities of the preceding Republican administration. Secretary Lawler cited statistics to show that the Leader administration eliminated unnecessary employees, developed job classifications, and prepared plans for the federal highway program. The administration concentrated on the construction of four-lane highways rather than smaller roads. Although they were more expensive, the larger highways were needed and the expense was offset by matching federal funds not available for the construction of two-lane highways.

TRAFFIC SAFETY
(A Bureau of the Department of Revenue)

Although Governor Lawrence is remembered for his dedication to traffic safety, the record shows that George Leader, too, was deeply committed to traffic safety. Before each holiday, he would plead with the people of Pennsylvania to drive carefully to avoid traffic accidents which would bring tragedy to the families gathered to celebrate the holiday. It was reported that Governor Leader wanted the State Police during the holidays to patrol in unmarked cars with their wives in the cars and with children's toys in the back window, to catch irresponsible drivers who endangered the innocent lives of other drivers and pedestrians.

In 1955, Pennsylvania's death toll from traffic accidents grew by 10 percent. The trend continued to increase in January and February of 1956. The administration then imposed mandatory rather than arbitrary license suspensions for speeding and other serious violations of the vehicle code. The public disliked these mandatory suspensions; however, they clarified the ambiguous law and reduced the number of work days state troopers lost in the courts trying to achieve the suspensions. The state's death toll declined thereafter to a point below the national average. The annual death toll in the state had peaked at 1,790 in 1956, but it dropped to 1,698 the following year, when the new suspension system was in full effect. The decrease in traffic accidents was recognized by the National Safety Council; it gave the state a citation for its traffic safety program. In addition, the legislature approved an administration-sponsored bill that required standards for truck brakes, in order to reduce the number of accidents caused by runaway trucks on Pennsylvania's mountainous highways.

George Leader established the Governor's Traffic Safety Council which suggested future legislation to improve traffic safety. The Council was chaired by Professor Amos Neyhart, who directed the Institute of Public Safety at Pennsylvania State University. Neyhart was a pioneer of the driver education movement, and his methods were used throughout the country and in Canada. Among the Council's recommendations was one of the most requested pieces of traffic safety

146

legislation: the use of radar to control speeders. Radar was used in neighboring states, and a test on the Pennsylvania Turnpike had proven radar's effectiveness in reducing fatal accidents. To the Governor's dismay, the legislature did not give authorization for the use of radar or for the use of another useful safety tool: the breath analyzer.

THE INTERSTATE HIGHWAY SYSTEM

During his campaign, Leader had promised to extend the state's turnpike system by expanding limited-access, four-lane highways in the northern area from New Jersey to Ohio and in the west from West Virginia to Erie. This idea was popular among groups like the Keystone Shortway Association and a committee in northwest Pennsylvania which wanted a new highway from Erie to Pittsburgh. Turnpike bills were passed early in the administration, and Leader thought that his administration would accomplish its goal.

However, the turnpike feasibility studies showed that new turnpike construction was not practical because there would not be enough traffic to make the roads financially solvent. As it was, the northeast extension of the turnpike was not self-sufficient and was being carried by the main line. Because the turnpike alternative was not feasible, Leader had no formula for providing new limited-access highways. They were too expensive to construct from the Motor License Fund alone.

The Federal Highway Act of 1956 enabled Governor Leader to achieve his campaign promise. This federal law authorized the construction of an interstate highway system for defense and emergency transportation. The financing of the roads was shared on a nine to one ratio, with the federal government matching nine dollars for every one dollar raised by the state. Under this agreement, the administration was able to convert all planned toll bridges, highways, and tunnels to free passage. The Fort Pitt Tunnel was one example; it was the last link in the Pittsburgh Parkway, which would be a major artery into and through Pittsburgh. The tunnel had already been designed with toll booths to collect funds to pay for its expensive construction. The administration

147

obtained approval from the Federal Bureau of Roads to add the parkway to the interstate system. It thus was able to obtain federal funding for the tunnel's construction and eliminate the need for tolls and traffic-slowing booths.

The Governor predicted optimistically that the Pennsylvania Turnpike would also become part of the interstate system. Federal funds would eliminate its existing debt and the Turnpike Commission and the tolls would become things of the past. Unfortunately, this never came to pass.

George Leader is also remembered for lifting the tolls from ten Pennsylvania bridges. These bridges, scheduled to have the tolls removed in 1961, were freed in 1957, because of the improved financial management of highway funds. Leader was convinced that the time for toll roads, bridges, and tunnels were to become things of the past, good only for causing traffic congestion and providing patronage jobs.

The interstate highways planned for Pennsylvania included an east-west road near the northern border. Route 6, a scenic route through a sparcely populated area, was to be converted into a limited-access highway. The Keystone Shortway Association criticized the location of the northern route and wanted the road more to the south between Sharon, near the Ohio border, and Stroudsburg, near the New Jersey border. This would result in the most direct thoroughway across Pennsylvania from New York City to Chicago.

The Association's study showed that it would cost ten million dollars less to construct the shortway than it would to reconstruct Route 6. It also gathered evidence to show that more people could benefit from the new highway because the central counties were more populated than the northern counties. Further, there would be less property damage incurred by building the shortway than by reconstructing the old road. Many people lived close to Route 6 while the new road would bypass populated areas. This evidence convinced the administration to press for the building of the shortway rather than the conversion of Route 6. The result was the construction of Interstate 80 which has brought increased industrial development to the center of the state, complementing the industrial development program begun during the Leader administration.

There was no interstate highway planned for the western part of the state to connect West Virginia, Pittsburgh, and Erie. Leader believed that this was an important highway route, especially in light of the upcoming opening of the St. Lawrence Seaway. A road from Pittsburgh to Erie would give the western area access to an Atlantic port and would encourage industrial development in the state's northwest. This route was one of the administration's turnpike plans; despite repeated efforts, Leader could not convince the federal government to support the north-south interstate.

One day, General Biddle, Adjutant General, called the Governor and told him that General Richard K. Mellon was at Indiantown Gap Military Base where the Governor had his summer home. Biddle suggested that the Governor come and talk with Mellon. During the conversation Leader brought up the subject of the need for a highway in the western part of the state. Leader thought Richard Mellon would be interested because of the Mellon's involvement in southwestern Pennsylvania. The Governor explained how he had tried to convince the Federal Bureau of Roads without success. The Governor urged Mellon to support this highway. Several months later, the Governor learned that the interstate between Pittsburgh and Erie had been placed on the masterplan. Some of Leader's associates criticized the planned highway, because it did not extend all the way to West Virginia. Leader optimistically believed that if they built that much of the road the rest would eventually be completed. The Governor was correct; Interstate 79 now connects Erie and West Virginia. The other main connecting interstate begun during the Leader administration was the Erie thoroughway connecting New York with Ohio. This road had already been designed as a turnpike, but was redesigned for interstate approval, to qualify for federal interstate funds for its construction.

Highway construction is one of the activities of state government which is never finished. Fifty miles of the new interstate system was constructed during the Leader administration, and another 100 were under construction. The administration's emphasis on quality personnel enabled the Department of Highways in subsequent administrations to accelerate the interstate program. There were only forty-four qualified engineers in the department in 1955, while there were 200 when Leader left office in 1959.

CHANGE OF COMMAND

For some time, Joe Lawler had requested the Governor to remove him from the post of Secretary of Highways, for reasons of poor health. In September 1957, Leader accepted Lawler's resignation as Secretary of Highways and appointed him to the Turnpike Commission, a less demanding position. Leader selected Lewis Stevens, a lawyer from Philadelphia, to succeed Lawler because of his integrity and administrative abilities. Stevens was active in civic and church activities and was part of the reform movement in Philadelphia government. In areas where Harral claimed that Lawler failed to implement the recommendations of the pre-inaugural study, Stevens did. In fact, he requested Harral to serve as chief deputy, a post whose creation Harral had suggested. The Stevens-Harral team raised the function of planning to the level of a separate department division. They also worked to put as many highway projects as possible into the construction stage. Highway construction was also part of the public works acceleration program to counteract the 1958 recession. Two thousand miles of highways were built apart from the interstate system; this set a record high for highway construction expenditures in the state.

Mary Jane Leader had been impressed with the number of roadside rests along California highways. She urged her husband to have more roadside rests built along Pennsylvania highways. The law permitted only one roadside rest per county, but as a result of Mrs. Leader's interest, the law was changed and more roadside rests were built. Seven hundred picnic tables were placed along the state highways to increase rest areas without the expense of acquiring land for roadside rests. The tables were constructed by prison inmates as part of the expansion of prison industry. The construction of roadside rests complemented the Governor's campaign for traffic safety, since they provided places for the fatigued driver to stop. They also were part of the Governor's program of highway beautification, a particularly strong interest for George Leader. He especially did not like billboards cluttering up the highways. "We need strong highway zoning legislation," he said, "to protect our highways and beautiful countryside from the squalid ugliness that mars so many of our roads."

Because of its political nature and its potential for misuse, the Department of Highways was constantly criticized by the public and the minority party. The legislature called for an investigation of the Department after the cinder scandals in 1957; George Leader contracted with the National Safety Council to conduct a comprehensive, non-partisan study of the department. The study's results were not favorable; but they could have been more damaging if some recommendations had not already been in effect when the study was released. Some Democrats in the administration did not want to release the report before the election, because they foresaw its use by the Republicans in the 1958 campaign, already underway. George Leader disagreed; to withhold the unfavorable report would be worse than its release. Despite its criticisms, he could point to many accomplishments already underway.

The primary recommendation of the report was the elimination of politics from the Department, especially from the personnel system. The report called for the enactment of a tenure law to ensure job security for all employees, a goal which still has not been reached in Pennsylvania. The Council recommended improvement in planning, a matter already addressed by Stevens and Harral; identified a need for legislation and administration action in other matters, such as right-of-way land acquisition, design and construction of highways, and traffic engineering.

The Department of Highways remained political, although somewhat less so during the Leader administration; nonetheless, improvements were made. The department was reorganized, jobs were classified, professionals were placed under civil service, and more professionals were hired. Construction levels reached record highs and the federal government's share in highway construction was increased.

TURNPIKE COMMISSION

The Pennsylvania Turnpike was begun in 1938, and the first stretch of new highway between Irwin in Westmoreland County and Middlesex in Cumberland County was opened in 1940. The last link of the east-west turnpike between Ohio and New Jersey was finished in 1954, while the northeast extension was under construction during Leader's administration. The Pennsylvania Turnpike was the first four-lane, limited-access road in this country. Its purpose was to furnish a well sloped, easily travelled and constantly maintained route across the mountainous terrain of Pennsylvania.

The turnpike was operated by the Turnpike Commission, an autonomous part of state government. It fell under no department control and was a self-sustaining entity. Revenues collected through tolls paid for its administration by the Commission, for the debt service, for the maintenance of the roadway, and for the support of the State Police who patrolled the turnpike.

The Turnpike Commission positions were considered political plums since they paid well for generally part-time work. The Commission was comprised of five members; the Secretary of Highways, and four members appointed for ten-year terms. George Leader had the unusual occasion to appoint all five commissioners to the commission, due to a large turnover after the turnpike scandals.

Leader appointed Franklin McSorley, a Pittsburgh contractor, to the Commission in 1955. A few months later, McSorley replaced Thomas Evans, whose term had expired, as chairman. John B. Byrne, a member of Philadelphia City Council, was appointed to the Commission in 1956 instead of Bill Green, whose nomination was withdrawn when it became apparent that the Senate would not approve his nomination. Because of irregularities uncovered in the Turnpike Commission, George Leader attempted to remove a number of the Commissioners, but the Pennsylvania Supreme Court decided that the Governor could not remove the turnpike commissioners without proof of wrong doing. Thus, Leader's attempt to remove David Watson failed. Because of the irregularities, Leader suspended McSorley and James Torrance. Both later resigned. Merritt Williamson, Dean of the College of Engineering at Pennsylvania State University, served for less than a year after the suspensions to form a quorum. James Trimarchi, an Indiana County businessman and politician, replaced Williamson and Joe Lawler replaced James Torrance.

MANU MINE SCANDAL

Early in the administration, Joe Kennedy, Secretary of Mines and Mineral Industries, received an anonymous letter alleging irregularities in the operation of the Turnpike Commission, especially in the current construction of the northeast extension. Normally anonymous letters were disregarded because they were usually unfounded or unjustifiable criticism of the administration, but this letter was convincingly genuine. Kennedy referred the letter to Lawler, who brought it to the Governor's attention. The administration's legal experts decided that the allegations warranted an investigation. Leader directed the Department of Justice and the State Police to investigate the Turnpike Commission.

The investigation turned up one of the most serious scandals in the history of Pennsylvania government. The persons involved, including Thomas Evans, Chairman of the Commission, attempted to swindle $20 million dollars. The instrument of this conspiracy was the Manu Mine Research and Development Corporation, composed mainly of Evans' relatives. This company had submitted an ambiguous contract, approved without question by the docile commission. From 1953 to 1956, the Manu Mine Company had collected some nine million dollars from the Commission; this sum comprised 95 percent of the company's total income. Imagine this sequence of events: first, the Manu Mine Company was hired by the Commission to study a potential *problem*; next, the company recommended that the Commission hire the Manu Mine Company itself to conduct a surface stabilization project for the new turnpike which was to cross over undermined land. Then the same company inspected its own operation, thereby concealing the unnecessary work it was engaged in and billing for. The work was confined to twelve miles of the northeast extension, and Leader explained that it cost the public about $26.00 an inch for the road, as a result of the company's activities.

The scandal resulted in the conviction of eight persons, six of whom went to jail. During the investigation, the Department of Justice uncovered other questionable activities involving the purchasing, selling, and use of turnpike vehicles.

As a result of the incident, Leader was convinced that the Turnpike commission had to be reformed. He proposed legislation to change the commissioners to non-salaried posts; because he wanted a Turnpike Commission whose members had little personal interest in abusing and perpetuating their political positions. As Leader said, "We need men who will free the Turnpike as soon as possible—in other words, men without a passion for the extension of their own jobs."

Leader was convinced that the days of toll roads were ended, and he felt that the turnpike should be removed from the toll system as soon as possible to keep Pennsylvania's roadways modern and competitive to nationwide traffic. The Interstate system did discourage the building of new tollways, but increased costs of maintenance strengthened the arguments for retaining tolls on the Turnpike and even supported increased tolls.

THE DELAWARE RIVER
JOINT TOLL BRIDGE COMMISSION

In Pennsylvania, routine transportation projects were financed on a regular basis from the Motor Vehicle Fund. However, some bridge and highway construction projects were too large to be undertaken and funded from the receipts of the Motor Vehicle Fund alone. For these larger projects, the state issued bonds to cover the costs of construction. Commissions were established as independent state entities to administer the facilities and collect tolls for repayment of the bonds.

Ordinarily the Delaware River Joint Bridge Commission would not have been important in any given administration. However, it became very important to the Leader administration. Certain circumstances caused the Department of Justice to investigate, and their investigation led both to the creation of the Division of Investigations in the Department of Justice and to a number of subsequent investigations.

Toll roads and bridges were popular political programs because of the patronage jobs they generated. The Delaware Bridge Commission, for instance, employed over 200 uniformed guards and toll collectors and had an annual operating budget of more than a million and a half dollars. The Commission was composed of ten persons: five from Pennsylvania, three ex-officio and two appointed; and five from New Jersey, three ex-officio and two appointed. The Commission operated five toll bridges and maintained eleven free bridges.

Joe Lawler, as Secretary of Highways, was automatically a member of the Commission. He told the Leader administration that the Commission's operational costs were excessive. A preliminary study of its operation by New Jersey and Pennsylvania officials uncovered sufficient evidence to warrant an investigation by the Department of Justice. This investigation found that the Commission operated in an extravagant and excessive manner and that public funds had been misused by several Commissioners.

The Commissioners served without salaries, but three Commissioners managed to obtain salaries for themselves by establishing an Executive Committee and paying themselves for serving on the Committee.

The Commissioners were entitled to receive reimbursement for their expenses related to Commission work, but abuses were uncovered here also. Not only were the expense accounts excessive, but also the Commissioners and some high level personnel filed more than once for the same expenses. Entertainment expenses bordered on the pompous and absurd, when for example, flowers were purchased to decorate the entire first floor of a hotel where a banquet was held to celebrate the opening of a new bridge. Also, salaries paid for top management positions were excessive when compared to similar positions in state government. The Chief

Personnel Officer of the Commission received an annual salary of $18,000. At the insistence of Joe Lawler, this amount was reduced to $7,500 comparable to salaries in the private sector. The individual resigned instead of accepting the lesser amount.

Politician favoritism was evident in a number of Commission actions such as the use of advertisement for the toll bridges. At one bridge there was a large billboard advertising the toll bridge, even though it was the only bridge in the area. The furnishings at the Commission's headquarters in Morristown, Pennsylvania were extravagant. Imagine oriental rugs and gold ash trays! The Commission used more than one kitchen complete with sterling silver flatware and a set of china with the Commission's seal imprinted on it. This last item was purchased for more than $4,000 from a company owned by one of the Commissioners.

Warrants for the arrest of five individuals, three ex-commissioners and two ex-employees were issued. Leader announced a one-third reduction in the Commission's 1956 operating budget to eliminate "fantastic salaries, unnecessary positions, and vague job classifications." The Commission was reorganized, and "featherbedding and extravagance" curtailed. Leader illustrated the excessive practices of the Toll Bridge Commission by noting that his administration had terminated 24 armed guards who guarded the free bridges "to prevent them from being stolen." The guards were supposedly stationed to enforce weight limits on the free bridges; however, many bridges needed no such protection.

THE DEPARTMENT OF BANKING

The Department of Banking preserves the state's financial stability by ensuring that banks and other financial institutions are secure and solvent; it gives the public the confidence to entrust their money to the banks. The role of the banking department was to protect the public by regulation and periodic inspection of the state chartered financial institutions.

The pre-inaugural study, done by W. Carlton Harris, professor of finance at the Wharton School, found that in general the banking department was running smoothly. The personnel was qualified, especially the bank examiners, who were required to pass an examination for the position. The examiners of the other financial institutions were also quite competent although they did not have to pass an examination for employment. Nevertheless, these employees still depended on political sponsorship to obtain their jobs, and occasionally, political sponsorship was more important than qualifications.

Despite the generally high level of expertise in the department, there were personnel problems. Many examiners were nearing retirement age, and some positions were vacant. Recruiting new examiners was difficult, because better positions were available in other states and in the National Banking Examination System, the Federal Reserve, and the Federal Deposit Insurance Corporation. These positions offered higher salaries and job security without the necessity for political sponsorship.

SELECTION OF THE SECRETARY OF BANKING

Pittsburgh's David Lawrence recommended Robert Myers[2] for Secretary of Banking; he believed that Myers met George Leader's criteria of quality and integrity. Lawrence knew Myers from the Earle administration, when Myers was a deputy Attorney General and later Earle's Secretary. Myers had left Pennsylvania politics, after the scandals which tainted the Earle administration. Myers had established a successful private law practice that specialized in banking cases.

George Leader discussed the position with Myers who was reluctant to accept the appointment because of earlier scandals. Myers told Leader that he would accept the position if he could retain all qualified department employees, regardless of their political affiliations. Through Myers' experience as a banking lawyer, he was familiar with many

---

[2]Lawrence later retained Robert Myers as his Secretary of Banking.

bank examiners, most of whom he considered true professionals.

Governor Leader was relieved not to have to fight with politicians about jobs in the Banking Department. However, matters did not work so simply. Shortly after Leader's inauguration, Secretary Myers had a confrontation with Bill Green, a well-known politician from Philadelphia. Green demanded the replacement of most, if not all, of the Republican bank examiners in Philadelphia. Even though the department was not very political, most examiners were Republican, because of the sixteen years of Republican rule. The Democrats could not understand why their long awaited chance to take over the state government should not eventuate in the customary spoils of victory. Since Philadelphia had a larger percentage of the state-chartered banks than the western part of the state, pressure for political positions was more intense in the east. Secretary Myers refused to accede to Green's demands and supported his position with Leader's promise. Green complained to the Governor, but Leader refused to break his promise to Secretary Myers that qualified employees would not be replaced for political reasons. Leader's action was a courageous political act, for the new Governor contradicted one of the major political powers in his party.

The Department of Banking was a self-supporting branch of the government. The revenues from its services covered the expenses of the banks and savings and loan association bureaus. Revenues from the small loan bureau also exceeded expenditures. The excess funds were contributed to the general fund. Most department work involved examination; thus, most of the employees were examiners. The bank examination bureau was the most important; it had branch offices in Philadelphia and Pittsburgh, each headed by a chief examiner. The savings and loan bureau had a branch office in Philadelphia but not a chief examiner; and the small loan companies were regulated by the Harrisburg office.

Only three general types of financial institutions were subject to department regulation: the state-chartered banks, the state-chartered savings and loan associations, and the small loan companies which included consumer discount companies, motor vehicle finance companies, pawnbrokers, and credit unions. All three types of companies were audited periodically to ensure financial solvency and adequate cash reserves and to identify any misuse of funds. The focus of the bank bureau was primarily preventative; while the role of the other bureaus was protective, i.e., guarding the public against illegal financial arrangements and interest rates.

The state-chartered banks continued to grow both financially and structurally during the Leader administration, with their total assets increasing by a half-billion dollars. The expansion of the banks through mergers and branch expansion was most noticeable; it became one of the major concerns of the Banking Department during the Leader years. Legislation enacted during the first session contained regulations which placed state banks in a more competitive position with the larger state and national banks. This facilitated more bank mergers and branch expansion, and removed bank stockholders from the process. The approval of the Secretary of Banking and the Banking Board was still required.

Personally, Secretary Myers did not like the rash of bank mergers that was taking place. Although he recognized that some mergers were necessary; he viewed the merger of larger banks with small community banks as an undesirable loss of financial autonomy and control on the part of local communities.

These mergers were often attempts by the larger city banks to expand their businesses into the smaller surrounding communities. For example, Bucks County began to expand in the 1950's. Levittown, the urbanization north of Philadelphia, was seen as a strong economic base by the Philadelphia bankers. They attempted mergers with banks in the area; where there were no such banks, they solicited branch offices.

Myers imposed more objective criteria for the establishment of branch banks. The law enabled a bank to open branches in adjoining counties. The location of branch offices was complicated by the dual federal and state banking system. National banks needed the approval of the Comptroller of the Currency for the establishment of a branch office, while the state banks needed the approval of the Sec-

159

retary of Banking. Often both national and state banks filed requests to establish branches in the same community. To allow all of them to establish branches could result in poor business opportunities. Secretary Myers stated that the relations between the Comptroller of the Currency and the Secretary of Banking determined the success of each system. During the Leader administration, there was a good working relationship, and the general rule for granting all branch approvals was a first come-first served basis. The net result of the mergers and branch offices among the state banks was 580 state bank offices in 1958: 24 fewer banks, but 73 more branch offices than in 1955.

The bank examiners were trained professionals, usually accountants or persons with banking experience. Because many of these examiners were ready for retirement, Secretary Myers sought a way to replace them. Myers found a competent chief deputy in Frank Poe, a banker from Pittsburgh, whom he placed in charge of recruitment. Instead of using the administrative personnel system, Myers proposed a program to attract qualified examiners to the department and asked the Pennsylvania Banking Association and the Savings and Loan League for their cooperation.

The plan, instituted in 1956, involved recruiting recent college graduates and placing them in a training program. The training consisted of sixteen weeks in a bank or a savings and loan association to familiarize the trainees with banking procedures. This training period was followed by on-the-job-training under the supervision of an experienced examiner. Under the program, thirty-one examiners were trained by the department. The Banking Department had the cooperation of the finance industry, which arranged the placement of trainees in banks and savings and loan associations. These institutions supported the program because they were aware of the need for competent management personnel in the banking industry. Secretary Myers believed that the examination field was good training for bank executives, and for this reason, he was able to obtain the cooperation of the banking industry.

The examiners of the Banking Department came under the executive board civil service when it was initiated in 1956.

The administration's effort to provide professional monitoring of Pennsylvania financial institutions won the respect of the state's financial community. Secretary Myers felt strongly that the financial institutions were of such importance to the state's economic security that they could not be examined by a political, unprofessional staff. The recruitment program and the extension of civil service status to the examiners helped tighten the bond of cooperation between the Department of Banking and the financial community.

Public relations was an important aspect of Myers' role as head of the Department of Banking. Previous secretaries concentrated on the banking industry and neglected the other financial institutions. However, the smaller institutions provided necessary, though different, types of services. Secretary Myers attended not only the annual meetings of the bankers; but also the meetings of the Savings and Loan League and the small loan companies. For the first time these smaller companies felt that they had a sympathetic ear in Harrisburg.

The first savings and loan company in this country was formed by people in Philadelphia pooling their ,pmeu' as a result they had the capital necessary to build homes. Even in the 1950's many of these savings and loans were very small, so small that Myers described them as having their stockholders' meeting in the kitchen of homes. The department encouraged these small state-chartered savings and loan companies to merge with larger companies in order to compete with the larger federal savings and loans associations. During Leader's administration, the number of savings and loans in the state decreased by 24 to a total of 709. The companies had combined assets of more than one billion dollars.

With some justification banks considered small loan companies as only a shade above loan sharks. On one hand, they would have liked to have seen them suppressed; however, they knew these companies performed useful roles in the state's credit system. The small loan companies were supervised by the Consumer Credit Division, run by O. B. Lippman, who was solely responsible for the fate of the small loan companies, probably because previous secretaries had not been too interested in them. The licensing of these small loan companies was done by Lippman and applications were usually approved. The department supervised 7,917 companies including vehicle financing and pawnbrokers. The small loan companies comprised the group with which Secretary Myers was most concerned.

In 1957, there were 900 small loan offices in Pennsylvania, 200 more than the combined total of offices in New York and New Jersey. These companies were concentrated in the state's populous areas, especially in lower income areas, where they often charged excessive interest rates, engaged in false advertising, and used coercive collection practices. Secretary Myers wanted to restructure the license procedure for small loan companies to include fiscally sound criteria for the establishment of new offices. Myers required the preparation of a population and economic study before granting a license for anymore small loan offices. Mr. Lippman was not pleased with the new procedures because he felt that his experienced judgement was sufficient; others felt that he had become too comfortable with common practices. The small loan companies were not pleased with the new regulations but they learned to accept them, and sometimes to circumvent them.

George Leader's political philosophy is apparent in the area of banking and credit, as it is elsewhere. His insistence on quality leadership and professional employees produced a department which placed public interest before party interest.

Developments in the banking and credit industry were changing the face, if not the character, of finance. The use of credit cards was increasing; most banks used personal service and "free checking" accounts to attract customers. The Department of Banking in the Leader years was small, but significant advances in the regulation of bank branching and small loan companies were made. The department staff worked for stability, careful development, and social responsibility of finance and credit institutions. Its achievements were not dramatic but necessary.

DEPARTMENT OF INSURANCE

The Department of Insurance, another regulatory agency of the state government, is similar to the Department of Banking, in that it consists mainly of employees who supervise the activities of one industry. Insurance is the largest industry in the country. It is involved in seemingly countless aspects of social activity, of which health, life, casualty, fire, auto, and unemployment insurance policies are the most obvious.

As in other departments, the pre-inaugural study uncovered many problems. For example, employees were grossly underpaid compared to similar positions in the insurance industry. The state's Chief Life Actuary was paid $7,300 while Fellows of the Society of Actuaries had salaries of $12,000 to $15,000 in the private sector. Organization was another problem; about 85 percent of Pennsylvania's insurance policies were written in Philadelphia, yet most of the department's employees were located in Harrisburg. The authors of the study, Dr. C. Arthur Kulp and Dr. Dan M. McGill, Professors of Insurance, suggested that more department operations be moved to the Philadelphia branch office. Moreover, although the department generated more money for the general fund than it expended, it had insufficient funds to carry out its functions properly.

SELECTION OF THE INSURANCE COMMISSIONER

In selecting the Insurance Commissioner, George Leader convinced the political leaders of Philadelphia to support Frank Smith for the post of Insurance Commissioner. They had originally pressed for his appointment as Secretary of Revenue. Smith had held many positions. He had been elected to Congress at the age of 27, was trained in the law, had been a U.S. Marshal and had worked for the Internal Revenue Service in Philadelphia.

Thomas Balaban was appointed First Deputy Commissioner. He was a lawyer from Green County, where he had served as legal counsel for a large fraternal order. Not surprisingly, he oversaw the fraternal insurance companies and personnel. Smith and Balaban easily filled positions using the traditional patronage system. The Insurance Department was the last department to be placed under executive board civil service; it was placed there at the Governor's insistence.

However, Commissioner Smith proved to Leader that he had the capabilities to run the Department. He followed the Governor's lead to tackle every aspect of insurance instead of just one or two, and combined hard work with quality people to produce what has been called the best insurance department in the state and possibly in the country. George Leader admitted that he had underestimated Frank Smith and regarded him as an excellent Commissioner. Smith's performance illustrates Leader's ability to bring out the best in people.

All insurance transactions in Pennsylvania were regulated by the Department of Insurance; a deputy oversaw each type of insurance. This state regulation consisted primarily of examining the insurance companies, licensing brokers and agents, and approving policies and rates. This final point was of particular importance to Commissioner Smith; he continually emphasized that the Insurance Commissioner did not *fix* insurance rates, but approved or disapproved rates fixed by the insurance companies.

Smith's major vehicle for improving the State's insurance industry was the public hearing. He held hearings on most types of insurance, and they were the first in the state's history. The hearings both provided information about insurance problems and stimulated public interest in insurance regulation.

The uninsured motorist was a growing problem in Pennsylvania during this time. Governor Leader ordered Commissioner Smith and Secretary of Revenue, Gerald Gleeson, to study the situation. The inquiry revealed that about 10 percent of the drivers in Pennsylvania were uninsured; they placed a substantial financial burden on insured motorists when the two groups were involved in automobile accidents. The Governor then called for a more comprehensive study, and formed a committee of citizens to examine the practices of other states and recommend changes.

The insurance industry resisted one solution to the problem, compulsory insurance, because they did not want to insure high risk individuals. An alternative is to insure motorists against uninsured drivers. Leader refused "to tolerate companies writing many hundred of millions of dollars of insurance premiums in Pennsylvania extending insurance protection against uninsured motorists in the state of New York, and denying such protection to the citizens of this Commonwealth." Responding to the administration's position some companies included the uninsured motorist coverage in their policies. Their efforts did not completely solve the problem, for the coverage was optional, and many people did not purchase the extra insurance, but it was a step in the right direction.

The Governor's Committee on the Uninsured Driver, chaired by Judge Crumlish of Philadelphia, reported its findings in 1956. The Committee recommended the certification of drivers as financially responsible before issuing them a license to drive, rather than after they were involved in an accident. This committee also suggested that all drivers be required to post a bond and that a fund, derived from a portion of the vehicle registration, be set aside to compensate the victims of accidents involving uninsured drivers. Four pieces of legislation prompted by this report did not pass during the Leader administration. In subsequent years, however, the problem was more satisfactorily resolved.

Insurance protection from floods was another area in which high costs deterred insurance companies from offering comprehensive coverage. Most assistance came from the federal government. After the devastating floods caused by hurricanes Connie and Diana, Leader formed a committee to investigate the flood insurance alternatives. Again, no action was taken for several years.

The health insurance companies received periodic rate increases without extensive scrutiny and with negligible opposition. Frank Smith began to conduct public hearings on these rate hikes. They uncovered several unaddressed problems with Pennsylvania's health insurance regulations, such as conflicts of interest between hospital officials and board members and the health insurance companies. The hearings also prompted the department to establish criteria for the operation of the health insurance companies.

In a famous adjudication prepared by Commissioner Smith, hospitals were instructed to economize their operations and to remove waste and abuses in the health insurance benefits. Upon recommendations of this adjudication, the Governor established a committee of forty-four persons to study the hospital system in Pennsylvania.

In 1957, the steel workers' contract added diagnostic coverage to its list of benefits. Leader praised this extension and said optimistically, "The public will benefit immeasurably by being able to receive this care at costs which they can afford. Such service will go far in alleviating physical and mental illness by early diagnosis and treatment."

THE PROBLEM OF THE MUTUALS

The mutual insurance companies were at this time basically post assessment companies. Their regulation became a particular problem in the 1950's. These small companies were often more like understandings among individuals in the community than formally structured insurance companies. The company collected premiums annually from its members to cover their incurred losses. In a good year, the premiums were low. In event of a larger loss, such as a barn fire, each member was assessed equally to cover the cost.

These companies were very useful in rural areas, and many were quite reputable. However, they were not regulated or required to maintain a cash reserve. Their agents and brokers were not licensed and their policies and rates were not subject to approval by the insurance department.

This lack of regulation invited fraud. Not surprisingly, unscrupulous individuals bought mutual company charters and moved their offices to the cities, where they wrote auto insurance as well as fire insurance. These fast dealers bid for the mutual charters at extraordinary prices, often higher than the value of insurance the company would write in a year. Since there were no state regulations for mutual companies, the new owners were free to write any insurance anywhere.

A rash of mutual company failures followed, which were directly related to the change in ownership. There was a pattern to these failures. The owners would move into a place like inner city Philadelphia and write insurance to high risk individuals at whatever premiums they could obtain. The company was organized under a management contract which would skim off at least half of the income. The first year or so, these companies would pay on claims. From the start, however, their policies often had excluding conditions such as traffic violation invalidating the auto insurance. These companies rapidly developed a high volume of insurance in low income areas, but usually in the second year they began delaying the payment of claims. Subsequently, they would stop paying altogether. The operators would then declare bankruptcy, having taken its profits through the management contract.

The insurance department was unable to effectively liquidate these companies and bring legal action against them. By law, the Division of Liquidation was funded from proceeds derived from the sale of the bankrupt companies' assets and from debts owed to them. Many of these failing companies had been looted so effectively that not enough money remained for the department to begin legal proceedings and recoup the outstanding debts. The pre-inaugural study had recommended an appropriation for the Liquidation Division so that it could properly pursue these cases and reclaim the losses. To prevent business failures, the Department provided special training for its examiners that helped them to identify signs of impending bankruptcy. The department subsequently filed criminal charges against some of the failing mutual companies; legal action helped deter other companies from engineering bankruptcy deliberately.

Regulation of mutual insurance companies would appear to be the simplest solution. It was surprisingly difficult to attain since the mutual companies resisted regulation. Reputable companies claimed that their operations and practices were adequate. They did not welcome compliance with insurance regulation such as maintaining cash reserves and licensing their agents. Strong rural Republican interest in the Senate added to the complexity of obtaining control of the mutuals.

Nevertheless, two acts were passed during the Leader administration, one of which required mutuals of a certain size to maintain cash reserves. This law allowed the small mutuals to retain their informal character. The second act regulated post assessment conditions, so that there could be no assessments without a prior agreement. Legislation was enacted during the next administration that firmly established the regulation of the mutual insurance companies in Pennsylvania. Governor Lawrence appointed Frank Smith as Insurance Commissioner; the work begun during the Leader administration came to fruition, not only in the area of the mutual insurance but also in other areas as well, under an administration with a more cooperative legislature.

Even though the mutual industry resisted regulation, they benefitted from it in the long run. These companies which had been small and vulnerable now rose to take their place alongside the commercial insurance companies in Pennsylvania.

OTHER AREAS

Another problem area in the insurance field identified by the professionals in the department was a frequent overcharge on insurance premiums because of misclassification of motorists into high premium categories. Since 1950, fifteen insurance companies affiliated with motor vehicle finance companies were found to have overcharged 36,000 Pennsylvanians about one million dollars. The Insurance Department discovered the irregularity during its routine examinations. The finance companies requested that the overcharge be paid to them, but Commissioner Smith insisted that the refunds be paid directly to the overcharged individuals.

The hard working employees of the insurance department were praised for their dedication and received national recognition for their achievements. Frank Smith attributed part of their success to their "cabinet meetings." These meetings were informal work sessions where the deputies shared their problems with the other deputies and the Insurance Commissioner. During the second half of the administration, Attorney General Thomas McBride joined the "cabinet meetings"; his presence added a new dimension to the meetings because the Attorney General became directly involved in many of the discussions and was able to add the weight of his office to the problem solving process. They were called "cabinet meetings," because Frank Smith opened the cabinet in his office and offered the staff a drink while they continued their after-hours discussions. The Governor stopped by one night to find out why the lights were on so late. Wasting energy? Not at all, the office was charged with energy—the insurance staff working at a "cabinet meeting."

Under the direction of Commissioner Smith the department was regarded as one of the nation's best. Its achievements were evident: new regulations, new legislation, and national recognition for their work. When Smith testified before state and federal hearings he modestly asserted that while the department was not the best in the nation, it was second only to New York's elaborate insurance department.

LIQUOR CONTROL BOARD

The Commonwealth of Pennsylvania has been and remains the largest single wholesale purchaser of alcoholic beverages in the world. Other states, such as Iowa, West Virginia, and North Carolina, have state-controlled operations similar to those of Pennsylvania, however, Pennsylvania's system is the largest because of the size of its population. The Liquor Control Board, established in 1934, regulates and controls the sale of all alcoholic beverages in the state. Except for beer and ale, it is also the sole distributor of alcoholic beverages. In the 1950's, the wholesale and retail operation consisted of over 600 retail stores, three warehouses, and more than 5,000 employees. The Board issued about 32,000 licenses per year to persons involved in the production, transportation, and sale of alcoholic beverages.

The Liquor Control Board did not receive an appropriation from the legislature, since it operated with money received from sales and fees. The state system generated a profit of about 40 million dollars yearly for the General Fund. The employees of the Liquor Control Board were by law civil service employees, except for the three commissioners appointed by the Governor.

Dr. Nelson McGeary, professor of political science at Pennsylvania State University, did the pre-inaugural study of the Board and found that the functioning of the Liquor Control Board was generally adequate. The roles of the Secretary of the Board and the Board itself were not clearly established. The Secretary worked for the Chairman of the Board, who handled administrative matters. However, this relationship was not fixed by law or regulation; for this reason, McGeary urged that the positions of the Chairman as administrator and the Secretary as his representative be defined legally.

Appointment to the Liquor Control Board was considered a political plum and was sought by many people. The Governor recalled that one person offered him unlimited campaign support for the rest of his political career in exchange for an appointment to the Board. But Leader would not appoint anyone to the Liquor Control Board who eagerly sought it or anyone whose motivations he held suspect. Instead, he chose persons whom he believed to be above reproach, and who also had business or administrative experience to make them qualified to supervise such a large merchandising and control operation.

Patrick E. Kerwin, an attorney from Dauphin County, was appointed by George Leader as Chairman of the Board. Kerwin had been chairman of Leader's primary campaign and it was rumored that he had been considered for the position of Secretary of the Commonwealth. In addition, Leader appointed Kerwin to his Cabinet. Donald A. Behney, a Republican, who had served as an employee in different capacities in the Board including secretary to the Board since 1934, was appointed by Leader in the first months of the administration. He was replaced two years later by Daniel Swaney, an educator from Fayette County.

Leader also chose John Rice, a loyal, well respected Democrat, to serve on the Board. Rice, a retired businessman, was a trustee of the Gettysburg Lutheran Theological

170

Seminary. Not surprisingly there were some questions about Rice serving on both boards, because of the religious group's feelings about alcohol. Seminary officials consented, believing that religious people should accept public positions of responsibility. When Rice later resigned to become Secretary of Property and Supplies, Leader appointed Abraham D. Cohn to the Board. Cohn was a retired businessman from York County; he had operated a successful clothing store until his early retirement. Cohn remained a member of the Liquor Control Board during the administrations of Leader, Lawrence, and Scranton, becoming the chairman in 1961.

As Chairman, Cohn pioneered several improvements in the Liquor Control Board. He introduced the LCB cards, ran a public information campaign on moderation in drinking, and placed a number of state stores in shopping centers.

During the Leader administration, the Liquor Control Board increased its number of stores from 614 to 640, remodeled or relocated a large number of old stores, and increased revenue and profits. Leader attributed these successes to his careful selection of honest and qualified persons for the board. Good management and business techniques minimized some of the problems of alcoholic beverage regulation. Leader's contribution was the fostering of efficiency and honesty into what has been a highly political operation.

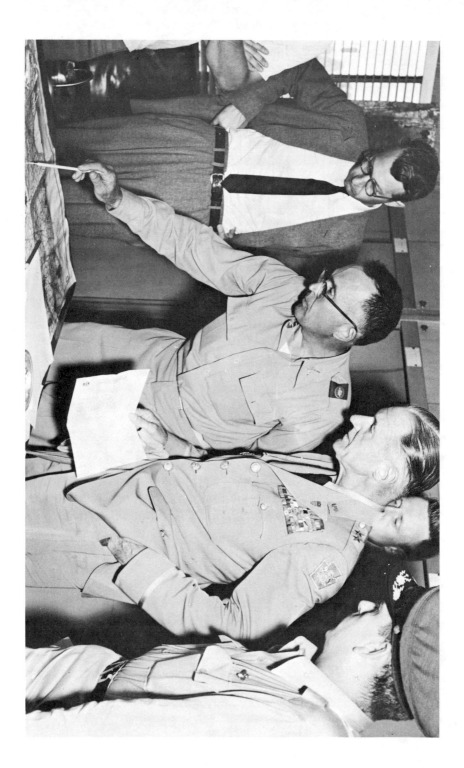

Chapter 6

The State

THE DEPARTMENT OF STATE

The Department of State is the oldest department of Pennsylvania state government and the Secretary of the Commonwealth, the head of the Department of State, was traditionally awarded to a strong political supporter and party leader. The Department of State was the legitimate political department of any administration. The secretary served as the governor's principal party connection and political advisor.

The pre-inaugural study, done by Albert B. Martin, Professor of Political Science at the University of Pittsburgh, found that the operation of the Department of State was fairly efficient. Martin's report was descriptive rather than analytical and problem oriented. The formal duties of the Secretary of State were both ceremonial, such as guarding of the State seal and flag, and practical, such as keeping the Governor's minutes and official state documents and punctuating and compiling the legislation of each session. The Secretary of State was also the official representative of the Governor for political and official matters of the state.

The Department of State was divided into four bureaus. The Bureau of Elections and Commissions was responsible for all election procedures from the filing of candidates' petitions to the compiling of election returns. All commissions of the state officials (judges, notaries, board members, etc.) were channeled through this bureau. All criminal extraditions originated here. The Corporation Bureau issued charters for corporations; its approval was required before a corporation could do business in the State. The Legislative Bureau was responsible for punctuating legislation, delivering it for the

Governor's signature, and compiling the signed acts in the state's pamphlet laws. The Administration Bureau microfilmed records, prepared correspondence, financial papers, and certified official documents.

The Secretary of the Commonwealth served on a number of boards, including the Board of Pardons. The retirement systems of municipal employees, state police, and state employees were in this department and the Secretary was a member of the three retirement boards. Because of changes in these systems, the number of employees covered under these plans increased greatly during Leader's administration. Public school teachers were permitted to transfer from their own retirement systems to the state employees retirement system, which was integrated into the Federal Social Security System. These improvements in the retirement system were part of Leader's attempts to enhance state employee benefits and to attract qualified people in all departments.

Efficiencies were introduced into the department's operations with the assistance of the Office of Administration. Despite an increased workload in the Corporation Bureau because of new legislation requiring the department to update all of its records, the department was actually able to reduce its work force by 20% because of improvements in its operations. Old and unneeded records were destroyed and more than 100 forms were simplified. New microfilming procedures also improved the department's recordkeeping.

SELECTION OF THE
SECRETARY OF THE COMMONWEALTH

Governor Leader followed political tradition in the selection of the Secretary of the Commonwealth and appointed James A. Finnegan, a Democrat from Philadelphia. Finnegan had held many government posts including that of the Secretary of the Delaware River Navigation Commission during the Earle administration. He was President of the Philadelphia City Council at the time Leader called him to Harrisburg.

Finnegan resigned in December of 1955 to become Adlai Stevenson's campaign manager. Leader considered his departure a loss for his administration because of Finnegan's political abilities. Because Leader was a strong supporter of Stevenson in his bid for the presidency, he willingly accepted Finnegan's resignation. After Stevenson lost to Eisenhower, Finnegan returned. In his absence Henry Harner, the deputy secretary of the Department of State, served as Secretary of the Commonwealth.

Finnegan was actively involved in national politics and was a member of the Pennsylvania delegation which Leader led to the 1956 Democratic National Convention in Chicago. At the convention, Finnegan informed Leader that he might be able to place Leader's name in the nominations for vice president. Leader declined the offer, explaining that he had plenty to do as Governor of Pennsylvania (this was shortly after the long legislative session and tax battle) and he had just come from the doctor the day before coming to Chicago. Leader had come down with hepatitis as a result of overwork. The doctor gave him a clean bill of health for the first time in weeks. Leader later regretted that his refusal ended his chances for national politics since the nomination would have given him nationwide exposure.

James Finnegan died in March 1958 and William Trout became Acting Secretary of the Commonwealth. Leader then asked John Rice to fill in as the Secretary of the Commonwealth for the last eight months of the administration. Rice took over in June 1958 and finished out the term.

STATE ATHLETIC COMMISSION

In the reorganization of the state's executive branch, the State Athletic Commission became part of the Department of State, rather than the Department of Revenue. This Commission was responsible for enforcing regulations at boxing and wrestling matches in the state. Governor Leader removed the previous members of the Commission because he wanted his own people on the Commission. He appointed James H. Crowley as chairman. Crowley had received his law degree from Notre Dame University where he had been one of Rockne's legendary "Four Horsemen." Prior to the Second

World War he had coached football at several colleges. Crowley was engaged in both television and the coal business when Leader approached him in 1955. Alfred M. Klein, Leader's second appointment, was a distinguished Philadelphia lawyer and writer who had investigated allegations of organized crime influence and racketeering in boxing. Leader's third appointee was Paul Sullivan of Pittsburgh.

Governor Leader suspended all boxing in Pennsylvania for 90 days in May 1955, after a match in Philadelphia generated claims of fight fixing. Subsequent investigations and hearings on abuses in boxing revealed that one of the fighters had been drugged. Other incidents concerning the physical condition of fighters, conflict of interests between promoters and managers, and racketeering were uncovered.

Leader asked the Pennsylvania General Assembly for new legislation regulating boxing and wrestling. Leader pointed out that the existing law had been enacted in 1923, and that these sports had been substantially changed since the expansion of media coverage. The financial picture had also changed; fighting had become big business. Speaking of the fighting sport, Leader observed, "home television, razor blades, and bottled beer are part of Wednesday and Friday evenings of millions of our people who have never been near a rosined arena." Leader contended that big business and big sports required government regulation.

While the legislation developed by his administration was being considered in the legislature, Leader addressed the National Boxing Association in Detroit and called for a uniform boxing code. Deputy Attorney General Harrington Adams was sent to the National Council of State Governments, and chaired a subcommittee to develop a uniform code.

The day the 90 day boxing suspension was to end, Leader extended the suspension until the legislature passed the new State Athletic Code. At the end of August, the code was signed into law and the suspension was lifted. The State Athletic Commission was given the power to enforce regulations in boxing and wrestling. This, Leader claimed, would raise the sport to the true level of acceptance in the public eye once again. Work continued on the uniform code, but it was years before anything was accomplished.

The elimination of racketeering in athletics was one of the code's purposes, and Leader's position was clear. Leader angered Democratic party leaders in another area with his dislike for gambling. There was to be a referendum on horse-racing, but the press began to interpret Leader's support for the referendum as support for the legalization of pari-mutuel betting on horse racing. He favored the referendum as an attempt to discern the public view; however, because of his personal dislike for gambling and the misinterpretations of his position in the press, he withdrew his support for the referendum, and the measure failed.

CIVIL SERVICE COMMISSION

The Civil Service Commission of Pennsylvania was established in 1941 to provide merit system personnel for those departments which by law required such personnel. The commission supplied employees for the Department of Public Assistance, the Bureau of Employment Security, and for the Liquor Control Board, and it administered examinations for state police applicants. But the civil service accounted for only a minor fraction of the total number of state jobs; the rest were controlled by the patronage system. Of the some 64,000 positions in Pennsylvania state government when Leader took office, only 14,000 were under civil service. New governors were responsible for filling about 50,000 positions when the parties changed, most of these employees were replaced. Many positions were filled through the Governor's personnel office from applicants identified and sponsored by the county chairmen. Other positions were reserved for the county chairmen, usually in the Department of Highways and Welfare. Top administrative positions were appointed by the Governor himself.

Leader identified three levels of state employees: (1) policy makers, including the department heads, deputies, and similar management personnel; (2) mid-level positions, those professional and technical persons whose skills were essential to the operation of the state government; and (3) positions which required persons who could be trained routinely for their job. The policy positions in the administration were naturally chosen by the Governor, and party affiliation and loyalty were factors. Lower level positions were most easily filled by patronage, "the cement of the party." The professional and technical positions often were vacant, because qualified persons could not be found due to job insecurity and a distaste for obtaining political sponsorship. The need for a merit system in some departments was apparent. The pre-inaugural studies prepared by professionals, rather than politicians, recommended some form of merit system to increase job security and improve the state's ability to recruit professional and technical personnel.

Leader tried to have civil service enacted through the legislature in both sessions but could not even get it past the Democratic House. The Democrats feared that civil service would keep Republican employees, instead of replacing them with Democrats who had waited so long and worked so hard for the opportunity to have those positions. The Republicans feared that the Democrats would be frozen into positions which they hoped would be theirs after the next election. To dispell these fears, Leader ordered a survey of the departments; of <u>those profe</u>ssional and technical persons appointed by the administration, 49% were Democrats and 51% were Republicans. This should have convinced anyone that civil service would not destroy the parties. Leader argued that the state desperately needed professional and technical people. Pennsylvania could not compete with private industry, other states, and the federal government without the job security and dignity of employment afforded through civil service.

As an example, Leader referred to the search for foresters. The Department of Forest and Waters needed 12 foresters to fill vacancies, but of the 50 graduates of the Penn State School of Forestry in that year, only *one* joined Pennsylvania state government. The others went mainly to other states where professionalism was respected and job security assured. The need for accountants, engineers, and mental health professionals likewise was not met because of patronage employment.

Prior to Leader's administration, the Civil Service Commission received little attention since its influence on the total state employment process was minimal. The Commission, however, took on new significance under George Leader, for he was determined to place as many professional and technical employees under civil service as possible.

The Civil Service Commission was a bi-partisan commission with three members. Leader appointed Dr. Elmer Graper, Professor *Emeritus* of Political Science at the University of Pittsburgh, and Miss Susan Baker of Lancaster County, a member of the League of Women Voters and a strong advocate of the extension of civil service, to the Commission. These two joined John McCarthy of Philadelphia who had been the minority member during the preceding administration.

The Executive Director of the Commission was Ralph Tive, a lawyer who had run Pittsburgh's civil service program. As Executive Director, Tive supervised the work of nearly a hundred employees of the Commission, who mainly received applications and conducted examinations. Tive found in the regulations that the Executive Board could approve the contracting of the Civil Service Commission by the departments to provide those departments with merit system employees. Tive presented this idea to the Governor who found it a viable way to, at least temporarily, place the professional and technical state employees under a civil service system.

Beginning in September 1956, the Executive Board authorized departments to contract with the Commission for civil service employees. Some of the first positions covered by the Board's order were accountants, engineers, and welfare personnel. Other positions were added later. Genevieve Blatt, Secretary of Internal Affairs and a member of the Executive Board, argued that some positions were policy positions and not technical ones. She was able to keep about 500 positions under the patronage system. While this first step did improve the state's recruiting abilities, employees had to be informed that their civil service status could be revoked by the next governor.

Leader's "Executive Board Civil Service" was the first step toward a true civil service system. During the Lawrence administration more positions were covered by civil service, and under Governor Scranton, a comprehensive program was approved by the legislature. Thus, slowly and grudgingly, the parties adjusted to a decrease in patronage positions and the realization that civil service is essential for effective government and not merely a way for the majority party to assure its members permanent state employment. This goal was not fully realized during the Leader years, but without Leader's use of the Executive Board option, the establishment of a merit system would have been delayed for decades.

DEPARTMENT OF REVENUE

The Department of Revenue was created in 1927 as the state's tax collecting agency; it was one of the largest departments, with over 3,000 employees. These employees collected over half a billion dollars annually for the state's operation.

The department consisted of nine bureaus, six of which collected tax revenues: (1) the County Collections Bureau (inheritance taxes and fishing and hunting licenses); (2) the Corporate Taxes Bureau; (3) Institutional Collections Bureau (fees for staying at state institutions); (4) the Sales and Use Tax Bureau; (5) the Liquid Fuel Tax Bureau; and, (6) the Bureau of Investigations and Collections. The Bureau of Motor Vehicles collected registration fees, and the Bureau of Highway Safety enforced the motor vehicle code and collected fines. There was also an Administration Bureau.

The pre-inaugural study, done by H. Michael Albers[1] of Pennsylvania State University's Institute of Local and State Government, strongly criticized the operation of the Department of Revenue. Partisan patronage and influence were not the only factors affecting the department's operation; the commitment and morale of its employees was also poor. The accounting department's procedures were archaic; although some business machines were used, most operations were still done manually. For example, envelopes in the Bureau of

---

[1] Michael Albers became director of the Bureau of Accounts of the Office of Administration.

Motor Vehicles, one of the world's largest mail order operations, were stuffed and addressed by hand. There were even
problems with space allocations with some bureaus jealously
guarding unneeded and unused office space.

SELECTION OF THE SECRETARY OF REVENUE

Democratic governors usually offered the position of Sec-
retary of Revenue to a Philadelphia politician selected by the
party. Thus, Revenue positions were filled by Philadelphians.
When Philadelphia politicians expressed their wishes to
Governor Leader about the appointment of the Secretary of
Revenue, he insisted on qualified candidates. They suggested
Frank Smith who headed the Internal Revenue office in
Philadelphia. Instead Leader appointed another
Philadelphian, Gerald Gleeson who established an impeccable
reputation for integrity as the U.S. Attorney in Philadelphia.
Frank Smith, however, was appointed Insurance
Commissioner.

In addition to collecting taxes and fees, the Department
of Revenue had its role in the budget cycle. Checks and
balances between the legislative and executive branches of
government are never more evident than during the budget
process when projected spending and revenue estimates are
like the rope in a tug-of-war. The executive branch over
estimated revenue so that the expanding state budget would
be approved; the legislature underestimated the revenue to
support its claims of overspending.

This was the situation in 1955. Governor Leader requested the legislature to let the Pennsylvania Economy
League analyze the state's financial position and submit a
figure that both the administration and the legislature could
use as a base for discussion.

One problem in obtaining accurate revenue estimates
was the archaic accounting system used in all departments.
While the administration tackled the whole problem, the
Department of Revenue was in so critical a condition that
very early in the administration, two accounting firms,
Laventhol, Krekstine and Company, and Price, Waterhouse
and Company were hired as consultants to modernize the
Department of Revenue's collection and control procedures.

The seriousness of the problem was stated in the agreement between the state and the consultants:

> because of the accounting weaknesses which have heretofore been present, there has been no certainty that the Commonwealth was actually collecting all revenues owed to it. And there has been no certainty that the collections have been as prompt as they should have been.

Improvements in the state's accounting system began in the second month of Leader's administration, not solely because of the pre-inaugural study, but because previous studies in 1950 and 1953 had also called attention to the dire need of modernizing the Department of Revenue's accounting procedures.

In Leader's first year, an administrative-sponsored bill allowing the state to invest inactive funds became law. This not only produced increased revenue through earned interest, but also significantly reduced the number of state bank accounts from 125 to 23.

The new accounting procedures did not solve all the problems in the Department of Revenue, but it eased them somewhat. The state had relied heavily on taxes collected from corporations. Even the temporary 1 percent sales tax imposed during the Fine administration did not substantially reduce the state's dependence on corporate taxes.

George Leader inherited a deficit of more than 52 million dollars and mandated increases and new programs brought the state revenue short-fall to 480 million dollars. The 1 percent sales tax was due to expire, and Leader had promised not to continue it. When asked about a new tax, Leader would state simply that several options were being studied. The tax that the administration finally proposed was the classified income tax. It would have taxed persons at different percentages depending on how they derived their income; wage earners would have paid 1 percent, professional and business income would have been taxed at 2 percent. Persons deriving their income from interest, rent or royalties would have paid 4 percent. Dividends were to be taxed at 5 percent, and on long-term capital gains, the tax would have been 6 percent.

Leader lost the tax battle. His classified income tax passed the Democratic House, but not the Republican Senate. Instead, it sent Leader a sales tax which he was forced to sign to prevent bankrupting the state. He realized that every day that he waited the state lost needed revenue, rather than waiting ten days for the bill to become law; Leader signed it.

The 3 percent sales and use tax was enacted in 1956 and amended shortly thereafter. It changed the state tax dependency from corporate taxes to the new sales tax. The bill took effect immediately, and it compounded the problems of the Department of Revenue. Secretary Gleeson called the tax the "most unenforceable sales and use tax law to be found anywhere in the United States." The tax was difficult to enforce because of exclusions built into the law. Some industries were exempt from the tax and many items were not taxable.

Although the Department of Revenue had a Sales and Use Tax Bureau with experience in collecting the temporary 1 percent tax during the Fine administration, the bill created an entirely new tax law. Both the public and merchants had to be taught the complex law, and new investigators and collectors had to be hired to collect the tax. The Bureau of Management Methods in the Office of Administration worked to improve the Bureau, but this was not enough.

The Governor again called upon experts to assist the Department of Revenue. A number of sales tax experts from around the country, including Dr. Luther Gulick of McKinsy and Co., assisted in the reorganization of the Bureau of Sales and Use Tax in order to improve tax collection. Their first recommendation was to increase the number of investigators and auditors. Stricter scrutiny would ensure proper enforcement of the new tax. To achieve this, the bureau needed twice as many employees; finding over 200 accountants and auditors was not a simple task. The consultants stressed the need for a merit system for these new employees if the state was to find the qualified people which it needed to make the new tax work. The executive board civil service placed accountants and auditors under the merit system for this purpose, but the Governor continued to ask the legislature to expand the State's merit system.

One evening Paul Smith, Director of the Unemployment Compensation Fund, overheard the Governor referring to the need for hundreds of accountants and auditors in the Revenue Department. Paul Smith leaned over and told the Governor that Allen Sulcowe, Director of the Employment Security Bureau in the Department of Labor and Industry had available all the accountants and auditors that the Governor needed. Leader approached Sulcowe on the matter the next day. Sulcowe explained that the accountants and auditors in his Bureau were paid from federal funds and could not be transferred, however, their services could be purchased. This was done and Sulcowe also conducted studies within the Department of Revenue in an effort to improve its operation.

The sales tax was not the administration's only tax problem. The corporation tax was also mishandled. Employees in the Bureau of Corporate Taxes actually recorded debits and credits in ledger books. There was no way of knowing who paid what, except to go to the books and check. A consultant had encouraged the administration to mechanize the corporate tax records, to improve the process. However, the automated system, after installation and operation, was not performing properly. Sulcowe's investigation of the operation found that there had been no way automatically to purge the files of accounts which had been paid. In effect, the system was totally useless, since there was no way of keeping accounts current except by manually adjusting the files. The bureau returned to the manual method until the automated system was corrected.

THE BUREAU OF MOTOR VEHICLE AND HIGHWAY SAFETY

The Bureau of Highway Safety was part of the Department of Revenue because it collected fees for violations of the motor vehicle code (see highways).

In an attempt to improve the motor vehicle registration process, the administration stopped issuing new steel license plates every year and instead issued a five-year aluminum plate with attachable validation tags for each year. The decision to use aluminum plates was based primarily on a reduction in mailing costs for validation tags. The change saved the state over a million dollars over the five-year period.

CHANGE OF SECRETARIES

Secretary Gleeson was an honest man, but not the strong administrator that Leader needed to deal with the problems in the Department of Revenue. It was reported that the Governor himself began working with the revenue staff. He promoted Gleeson to a judgeship in Philadelphia in January 1958. Leader selected Vincent Panati, the attorney who had been in charge of the Manu Mine case in the Turnpike Commission to replace Gleeson.

Unfortunately, Panati died three months later. Leader then asked Sulcowe to become Secretary of Revenue, because he had grown so familiar with the department's operation. Sulcowe declined the post because he did not want to lose his civil service status in the Employment Security Bureau. He did agree to serve as Acting Secretary until the end of the Leader administration.

The Department of Revenue had many problems when Leader entered office. By professionalizing the staff, improving management methods, and modernizing accounting and control procedures, the department improved the state's revenue collection.

DEPARTMENT OF JUSTICE

Appropriately, the Department of Justice was one of the most professional departments of the Pennsylvania State government. This is not to say that the department was not political, but rather that its employees were professionally trained because of the nature of their work, since they were mostly lawyers. Nevertheless, the department was staffed by patronage, for the party in power selected the Attorney General and also the deputy attorneys general.

Basically, the Attorney General and the Department of Justice served as legal counsel for the Governor and the state with the power to investigate and prosecute violations of state law. They also advised the governor on the legality and value of proposed legislation, and helped to draft legislation for submission to the General Assembly.[2]

SELECTION OF THE ATTORNEY GENERAL

The new Governor did not have difficulty selecting his Attorney General. Leader chose his political mentor, Herbert Cohen, a strong political force in Leader's home county of York. Cohen was no newcomer to state government having served four terms in the state House of Representatives, beginning in 1933 when he was the majority leader. Later, he was head of the Legislative Reference Bureau. Cohen was the president of the York Bar Association when Leader appointed him Attorney General. Cohen chose a young lawyer, Harry Rubin, to be his chief deputy.

Although some deputies were replaced in the transition, for the most part, the new administration retained competent persons. This was done despite protests from Democratic party leaders. Democrat David Lawrence was not happy with the retention of Deputy Edward Friedman, a Republican who had participated in the investigation of the Earle administration. Lawrence had been tried but found innocent of charges stemming from that investigation; he wanted Friedman fired for his role, but Leader and Cohen would not do so.

The Department of Justice and the Pennsylvania State Police were authorized to investigate alleged misconduct in state government. This power, though used in the past, was never exercised as extensively as it was during the Leader administration; in fact, a new division for investigations was created in the Justice Department. It is not difficult for a party which had been in the minority for so long to have some indication of wrong doing by the members of the major-

---

[2]Governor Leader vetoed 170 bills during the two sessions that he was governor. By comparison, Governor Pinchot had vetoed 256 bills in 1931. Conversely, Governor Leader signed 1,128 bills into law during the same two sessions.

ity. This was the case when the Democrats came to power in 1955. In a number of instances, the Department of Justice investigated and brought charges against Republicans from prior administrations and those who were retained by the Leader administration. However, the unexpected was that this new administration did not tolerate corruption by anyone and searched out and found offenders in its own administration rather than protecting the individuals by doing nothing and letting the next administration deal with the problem. Attorney General Cohen stated that the administration would investigate all instances of corruption and illegal practices; "This administration will ferret out any persons who have been involved in corruption or illegal practices in awarding and receiving state contracts." Cohen declared that his office would review all contracts and prosecute any persons involved in criminal activity, "This administration will not tolerate any such activities by any person doing business with the state." The "cinder scandal" in the Department of Highways involved three Democratic employees appointed by the Leader administration, who held leadership positions in their own counties. Responding to charges that other Justice Department investigations were politically motivated, Leader stated that, "When any employee of this administration does wrong, he can expect to be held fully accountable to me." Regardless of party affiliation, the administration sought out and prosecuted instances of corruption.

In another case, party affiliation was not an issue for an employee who had been with the state for a number of years. He and two contractors were arrested for arranging contracts so that the contractors could rent equipment owned by the state employee. Politics was more apparent when the Department of Justice charged several prominent Republicans with using state-grown seedlings that were intended for reforestation, for personal use and profit. Cohen contended that the prior administration knew of the violations, but had dropped the matter because of the persons involved. No action was taken until the Leader administration. In another instance, a tax collector hired by the Fine administration was found withholding sales and use tax receipts from the state. He was immediately dismissed from his post and arrested for embezzling nearly $2,000. The most spectacular charges were exposed by the Justice Department during their investigation of the Delaware River Joint Toll Bridge and the Turnpike Commission. (See those sections.)

The Division of Civil Rights was created in the Justice Department during the Leader administration, after problems arose when a black family purchased a home in the new development of Levittown. The family's move into the all-white community precipitated hostile action which not only destroyed their property, but also endangered their lives. Leader was convinced that a small number of troublemakers were responsible; so he ordered the State Police to protect the family and the Department of Justice to file injunctions against certain persons.

The department collected debts in the public escheat account. All debts, taxes, and accounts due the state were referred to the Department of Justice after 90 days; when it became the department's duty to collect them. In 1937, during the Earle administration, the Reporting Act had been passed, but for the sixteen years of Republican administration, the law was virtually ignored. During the four years of the Leader administration the department collected millions of dollars on accounts that might otherwise have remained delinquent.

As chief legal counsel, the Department of Justice became involved in discussions about the constitutionality of Leader's proposed classified income tax. Leader wished that the state's courts could offer advising opinion on proposed legislation; however, they only can address cases brought before them. Imagine the state's problems if the tax were enacted but declared unconstitutional by the courts six months later, with an order to return the money. Discussions in the Department of Justice of the proposed tax were divided along party lines. The Republican deputies were convinced that the tax violated the uniform taxation provision of state constitution. The Democrats defended Leader's proposed tax, calling it a means of taxing all Pennsylvanians equally by categories of income. The proposal was obviously fair from certain social premises, but it was doubtful, however, whether Leader's tax was *equal taxation* within the intent of Pennsylvania's constitution. (Subsequent decisions during the Shapp administration would seem to indicate that it would have been constitutional)

George Leader appointed Herbert Cohen to the Pennsylvania Supreme Court in 1956. Leader asked Cohen to recommend a highly capable replacement. Cohen suggested Thomas McBride, who had an outstanding record as a trial lawyer in Philadelphia and was known as "the Lawyer's lawyer." He had been an advisor to Richardson Dilworth and was Chancellor of the Philadelphia Bar Association.

McBride served as Attorney General for nearly two years. When there was another vacancy on the state's supreme court, Leader appointed McBride. Although Cohen was elected to retain his seat in the next election, McBride lost his bid for an elected seat on the bench.

With only a few months remaining in his term of office, Leader appointed one of the deputies Acting Attorney General. He was Harrington Adams, who had joined the Department of Justice in 1939 under Governor James. Adams was considered one of the best constitutional lawyers in the state, and drafting legislation was his specialty. He was a member and former chairman of the Drafting Committee of the Council of State Governments.

BUREAU OF CORRECTIONS

During the Fine administration, the Devers Committee studied the state's prisons and made recommendations for reforms. In 1953 the legislature, prompted by the committee's report, transferred the Bureau of Corrections from the Department of Welfare to the Department of Justice. In addition this legislation established diagnostic centers, upgraded staff, and reorganized the prison industries. This was not the first prison reform in Pennsylvania. The first prison reform in this century came during Governor Pinchot's first administration when prisoners actually controlled the state penitentiaries. The prison system had deteriorated to the point where drug abuse and alcoholism were common. Alcohol production and prostitution actually took place inside the prison walls. The situation in Pennsylvania prisons in the 1950's was in no way as bad as it had been in the 1920's, but reform was needed. During the Leader administration, the Bureau of Correction, under the direction of Commissioner

Arthur T. Prasse, continued to implement the recommendations of the Devers Committee, especially in the area of prison industries.

Prison industries were not widely accepted by the public. Although it was better for prisoners to be involved in productive work than for them to be idle, strong lobbying groups opposed prisoners producing items that might take jobs and business away from citizens in the surrounding communities. Satisfying both interests was difficult. One successful project begun by the Leader administration was the construction of picnic tables for the state parks and highways. In addition to the prison industries, the Bureau of Correction and the Department of Forest and Waters established mobile forestry camps for juvenile offenders where they worked on forest projects.

BOARD OF PAROLE

The Board of Parole was established in 1941. This three member board, appointed by the Governor with the consent of the Senate, gave parole to inmates of the state's penal system and supervised those on probation. The Board processed over 3,000 cases per year (over 60 per work day) and was responsible for supervising approximately 6,000 parolees.

Like Leader's other commission appointments, his nominations for the Board of Parole were not acted upon by the Republican Senate until the middle of 1956. Leader reappointed Theodore H. Reiber. He had been appointed to the Parole Board in 1943 by Governor Martin and reappointed by Governors Duff and Fine. Reiber, originally of Pittsburgh, spent his entire public career in parole work.

Leader found a candidate for the chairmanship of the Parole Board in Germany and invited him to return to Pennsylvania to serve on the Parole Board. Paul Gernert had been the Warden of Berks County Prison for nine years prior to 1946. He was recognized as running one of the ten best county prisons in the country. Gernert obtained national attention when he was chosen to direct the confinement of Italian war prisoners during the Second World War. He subsequently supervised American prisons in part of occupied Germany.

Gernert's position in Germany was comparable to Chairmanship of the Parole Board, when Leader, without an interview, invited him to serve as Chairman of the Parole Board.

Gernert only agreed to return to Harrisburg because he was aware of Leader's efforts to remove politics from the state's correctional system. Gernert had been disgusted by Pennsylvania's politics when he was considered for the wardenship of a state penitentiary before the war, but was not selected because he was a Democrat. Leader's bi-partisan cabinet helped to convince Gernert that Leader was sincere. Leader also appointed a black minister from Dauphin County to the Board. The Reverend Richard T. S. Brown had been active in corrections work in Michigan before coming to Pennsylvania.

Because of the staff's heavy workload, the number of parole agents was increased. The average caseload was reduced from 73 to 69 per agent. In Philadelphia, however, even with the additional staff, the average caseload was 88 parolees. There was a problem recruiting parole agents, because of the low salaries offered by the state, compared to those in the federal government. The Board of Parole paid particular attention to training agents and to improving communications with the various levels of state law enforcement agencies.

BOARD OF PARDONS

The Board of Pardons consisted of the Lt. Governor, the Secretary of the Commonwealth, the Attorney General, and the Secretary of Internal Affairs. This Board had two elected officials and two appointed members, giving it a more objective stance than one comprised completely of the appointees of the Governor. The Board made recommendations to the Governor for pardons and commutation of sentences. Only the Governor had the authority to pardon or commute sentences, but he could not do so without the recommendation of the Pardons Board. The Governor was not obliged, however, to accept the Board's recommendations for clemency.

The Board of Pardons, which heard about a thousand cases per year, was related to the Board of Parole. The latter required a prisoner to serve at least 15% of his sentence before becoming eligible for parole. Someone who had a life term, because it is not a specific number of years, could not serve 15% of that term unless the Board of Pardons recommended, and the Governor concurred, that the sentence be reduced. After serving 15% of the reduced term, the person went before the Parole Board.

In most administrations, pardon and commuting procedures were seldom major news items and rarely politically controversial. However, during the Leader administration one particular case made that procedure, the persons involved, and the Governor both newsworthy and controversial.

In 1947, David Darcy and three others were convicted of armed robbery and murder, and three were sentenced to die. Darcy had lost several appeals. He asserted that he was unable to get a fair trial in the emotionally loaded county court. Philadelphia Democrat Matthew McCloskey supported Darcy, and it was commonly known that Darcy was a nephew of his political secretary.

The Board of Pardons of the previous administration had denied Darcy's appeal for clemency, but the new Board commuted their sentences to life imprisonment. Leader's policy was to accept the Board's recommendation, because he did not have the time or expertise to review all the cases. Leader, consistent with his policy, approved the Board's recommendation about the Darcy case.

Philadelphia Inquirer publisher Walter Annenberg highly publicized Leader's action and criticized Leader for turning criminals loose on the public. These allegations continued for the rest of the administration, and Leader did not respond, believing that the truth of the case would prevail. When the Republicans raised the commutation issue in the senatorial race, Leader offered statistics that showed that his Board of Pardons, and he as Governor, had been tougher than any other recent administration. A legislative investigation failed to uncover any political influence on the Board's decision.

DEPARTMENT OF PROPERTY
AND SUPPLIES

The Department of Property and Supplies functions in state government like the purchasing office in a large company. Governor Leader liked to compare state purchasing to the housewife's role of providing the necessities for her family within the tight confines of her budget. He often used this analogy to warrant the strict business practices of his administration. He said, "The state as well as the average family should be able to shop around to fill its needs effectively and frugally." Leader viewed his experience as a poultry farmer as a valuable business education. He believed that it distinguished him from previous governors, most of whom were lawyers with little business experience.

The pre-inaugural study done by Charles H. Frazier, a Philadelphia engineer, identified personnel problems here as in other departments, because of the preponderance of patronage employees. Patronage employees often meant *patronage purchasing* or purchasing for the benefit of political friends rather than the tax paying public. Although most purchases were not strictly illegal, they were wasteful, since quality materials were available at lower prices, had saving been the department's objective. One of the ways to bolster patronage purchasing legally was writing "specifications." For instance, if there was a need to buy chairs for the state, the purchaser could specify a design for chairs which only a favored supplier could supply.

SELECTION OF THE SECRETARY OF
PROPERTY AND SUPPLIES

In this department, George Leader made a political appointment, in order to balance his cabinet geographically. William Thomas, the county chairman of Mercer County, was appointed to the post. Leader had hoped that Thomas would fit this position well since he operated a large successful florist business. His appointment did not work out, however, and reports that Leader was dissatisfied with the operation of the department were followed by Thomas' resignation at the end of the administration's first year.

Democratic party leaders then suggested John Rice, whom Leader had appointed to the Liquor Control Board. Rice had served in the State Senate and had run unsuccessfully for governor in 1946. Joe Barr, State Democratic Chairman, recommended Rice as a person who could handle almost any administrative position. Leader appointed Rice who ran the department capably until the middle of 1957. He then requested Leader to accept his resignation so he could realize his long planned retirement.

Andrew Bradley was the person most acquainted with the Department of Property and Supplies, because the department comptroller reported to him. Leader asked Bradley to take the post. Bradley served the administration well in that position, eliminating the patronage purchasing problems that remained.

INSURANCE OF STATE PROPERTY

Insurance commissions were handled by the department, but Harvey Taylor was the person Democrats associated with them. Senator Taylor was reported to have obtained his political power through these commissions. Generated from the insurance policies on state property and employees, they amounted to a substantial sum each year.

Traditionally, the commissions were distributed on a patronage basis. Harvey Taylor gave commissions checks to faithful Republicans near election time. The checks were usually for $3,000, but at times, were more; they were used to finance Republican campaigns. Harvey Taylor also distributed insurance checks to some Democrats in leadership positions. Whether giving money to Democrats was an attempt to demonstrate that these checks were not for political purposes or a means to maintain some control over the minority party is unknown, but certainly, their effect was felt by the Democrats who ran against Republicans who received the checks.

Under a Democratic governor, the party expected the insurance commissions to be given to its candidates. This was not the case; George Leader wanted an administration above reproach, so he refused to have the insurance commissions distributed to Democratic politicians for political reasons as the Republicans had done. Instead, they were distributed to licensed brokers on a patronage basis, but none were given to members of the General Assembly or to any state official or employee. The commissions paid on insurance policies were automatic and required by law, so the State could not pay for insurance coverage without paying that part of the cost which was the commission. Some savings were achieved by reducing the percentage of the commission. Some commissions on state insurance policies ran as high as 25% to 35%; Leader reduced the rates to around 10% to 15%.

The Governor established a committee to study the state insurance system. Dr. Stephen Sweeney, Dr. Howard Teaf of Haverford College and Dr. C. A. Kulp of the Wharton School of Finance conducted an exhaustive study of the state's insurance purchasing practices and made recommendations that resulted in tremendous savings. They found that the State could actually increase coverage but reduce expenses by consolidating coverage and by eliminating patronage considerations.

Previously the State's 9,200 vehicles were covered by 1,900 policies. Many of these were single vehicle policies. This practice was inherently wasteful, not only in the cost of extra premiums, but also in the number of hours that state employees had to spend keeping track of several hundred insurance policies. By consolidating policies for the vehicles, the state was able to increase its coverage for more vehicles at a 17% savings, despite a general increase in insurance costs.

In another instance, the state bonded 3,000 state employees for $1,000 per person. As a result of the insurance committee's study, the state purchased a blanket bond for 40,000 state employees with coverage of $10,000 per person. This was a 74% savings over the prior limited coverage.

Clayton E. Moul was named as the broker of record responsible for insuring state property and employees. The economies realized through the reduced commission percentages and in improved purchasing practices saved the state $200,000 per year.

ECONOMIES IN PURCHASING

Pennsylvania owned more than 9,000 motor vehicles. A survey showed that many vehicles were not in use because they needed repairs, while others were so old as to be beyond repair. The practice had been to keep a car for up to ten years before replacing it with a new one. Cars were bought singly or in small groups at retail prices. Leader, following the example of other states, instituted a buying plan that saved the state money and provided safer cars for state employees. Rather than purchase cars individually at retail prices, the state began to buy cars in fleets of hundreds at wholesale prices. The cars were used for one year and then sold to the public at retail prices. This practice gave the state one year of almost maintenance free use at little or no cost, because the cars were sold for roughly the price at which they had been bought. This purchasing plan did not replace all the state cars at once because of budget limitations, and before it was implemented completely, the plan was modified by the next administration.

The Department of Property and Supplies also effected substantial savings in the area of medical and hospital supplies. The state purchased large quantities for its hospital and mental institutions. Prompted by a disclosure of irregularities during the previous administration, the Department of Justice conducted an investigation of medical and hospital supplies purchases. This investigation discovered political purchasing practices that cost the state an estimated one million dollars per year. Department employees purchased from favored suppliers, bought expensive name brands, and used cumbersome purchasing techniques. The department instituted new procedures upon the recommendations of the Office of Administration; they resulted in streamlined, bulk purchasing and where possible the use of generic products.

These modernized purchasing procedures saved approximately 10% of the state's $50 million dollars of annual purchases. These savings came primarily from insurance, automobiles, and medical and hospital supplies. Smaller savings were realized by improved purchasing of many ordinary supplies, printing a catalog of commonly purchased items, and by keeping an inventory of all items purchased for the state.

OTHER FUNCTIONS OF THE DEPARTMENT

The Department of Property and Supplies was responsible for the management of all state buildings. Three new buildings were added during the Leader administration, and the Secretary claimed that there was no increase in total management cost because of improved management and the elimination of unneeded employees.

The department was responsible for the new centrally-located computer which the Office of Administration believed would result in substantial savings for the state. The Univac computer made by the Remington Rand Company, installed in 1958, was the first central computer used by a state government. The first task assigned to the computer was the state payroll.

Under the Leader administration, the state adopted uniform standards for building materials, site development and construction design. A survey highlighted waste caused by an absence of standards which allowed individuals designing or planning state buildings too much discretion to use very expensive materials. These standards applied to state office buildings, state college buildings, school buildings, and state hospitals and institutions.

George Leader was convinced that Pennsylvania had not taken advantage of enough federal programs. He stated, "in the past two years, we have stepped up our efforts to secure for Pennsylvania a fair share of Federal assistance." This applied as well to federal surplus property. The state went from 46th to third in the amount of surplus equipment distributed to its schools, institutions, and hospitals. The budgets of these institutions went further, because the federal property was purchased at about 2.5% the original cost, which covered warehousing and freight costs.

The federal government made surplus food and equipment available to the needy and to schools, state institutions, and other non-profit institutions. Prior to the Leader administration, the distribution of surplus food was almost non-existent in Pennsylvania. The Department of Property and Supplies, responsible for the distribution, began to increase the number of people receiving surplus foods. At one time, 100,000 persons received food but the federal government considered this figure too high. It sought to raise the eligibility requirements in Pennsylvania, while the administration worked to keep people receiving unemployment compensation and social security on the surplus program. The number of recipients stabilized at 60,000 persons.

The philosophy of the administration was to economize wherever possible to free funds for important public needs. The new Office of Administration was deeply involved in reorganizing the state's purchasing procedures. Outside experts were used, as for the insurance study, where the administration did not have the expertise to handle the problems internally. Leader did his best to close the doors of temptation and opportunity to those who might have chosen to use them. Constant vigilance is the price of responsibly handling public funds. Leader was consistent in his efforts and a number of very tangible achievements, especially in purchasing efficiency, were apparent.

DEPARTMENT OF MILITARY AFFAIRS

The Department of Military Affairs dated back to colonial times and the Ben Franklin Associates. The office of Adjutant General was established in 1793; and was an unusual mixture of state and federal responsibilities. The department's head was the Adjutant General, a cabinet officer in charge of the Pennsylvania National Guard. The Guard consisted of about 20,000 men paid by the federal government as part of the national military system. The Guard was administered by the state until a national emergency warranted federal mobilizaton of the Guard. About 1,500 civilian employees in the department were also paid from federal funds. The state was responsible for over 100 armories that stored equipment and arms.

The Pennsylvania National Guard had a proud tradition and was one of the first guard units to be called in wartime. The Headquarters of the Guard and the Department of Military Affairs were at the Indiantown Gap Military Reservation.[3] This large comprehensive training camp, located north

---

[3]The Governor also had a summer residence at the Indiantown Gap Military Reservation, where Leader chose to reside during his first year in office and during the summer months thereafter.

of Harrisburg at the foot of the Blue Ridge Mountains was opened in the early 1930's. The Pennsylvania National Guard trained there when it was called to active duty during the Second World War. The reservation was used as a federal training installation during the Korean conflict and later as a training facility for the Guards of neighboring states.

SELECTION OF THE ADJUTANT GENERAL

The post of Adjutant General was traditionally a political appointment. In the past, low ranking military persons had been appointed and rose to higher levels of rank through state promotions which were not generally recognized by the federal military system. As in other departments, George Leader wanted a qualified person to head the Department of Military Affairs. Anthony J. Drexel Biddle[1] was considered by the Democratic party leaders as a person well qualified for the position of Adjutant General.

Biddle was, at the time of his appointment, a General in the regular army and had an exceptional career as a diplomat and a military man. He served as a minister to Norway (1935–37) and to Poland (1937–39). He had been Deputy Ambassador to France in 1940, and Ambassador extraordinary to the exile governments of Poland, Belgium, the Netherlands, Norway, Greece, Yugoslavia, and Czechoslovakia from 1941 to 1944. He served in the U.S. Army as a captain in 1917–18 and reentered active duty in 1944. General Biddle served in various positions including Special Assistant to General Matthew B. Ridgway, U.S. Army Chief of Staff.

A. J. Biddle was appointed as Adjutant General in April 1955. George Leader considered him a real asset to the administration because he had the respect of the federal military establishment and foreign affairs experts. Biddle was one of Leader's chief advisors, especially in areas relating to the federal government, foreign affairs, and national defense; areas to which Leader often addressed himself, as Governor of the third most populous state in the nation, as Commander in Chief of the Pennsylvania National Guard and later as a candidate for the U.S. Senate.

---

[1]General Biddle was reappointed as Adjutant General by Governor Lawrence.

An example of how General Biddle was able to use his extensive military experiences for the administration was in attempts to attract defense industries to the state. Early in the administration, Biddle acquired an early copy of the relief maps that he had helped develop before coming to Harrisburg. These maps were used by the Departments of Military Affairs and Commerce to convince defense industries to establish defense industry plants in Pennsylvania. The mountains and valleys were said to provide natural defense barriers against nuclear attacks. It was asserted that only a direct hit would be effective, since the shock wave would be deflected by the mountains. Although other states had similar mountain ranges, no state had the large number of flat valleys, coupled with access to good land and water transportation, nearby cities, and ample labor supplies.

Members of the Leader administration remembered General Biddle as a gracious and charming man. He was a politician and a professional, and at one time, he was considered by Pennsylvania Democrats as a possible candidate for governor.

THE PENNSYLVANIA NATIONAL GUARD

The Guard had two purposes: to defend the state in time of war or local emergency, and to serve the nation as a trained military reserve in case of war. The National Guard had about half the strength of the regular army. Yet the Guard was often belittled by the federal military system because of its frequent political entanglements. The National Guard had traditionally been a dumping ground for outmoded weapons and equipment. However, with the ever-present threat of attack in the new atomic age, the Guard was held in more esteem. Governor Leader announced to the public that the federal authorities proposed to provide the Guard with defensive weapons to protect the state, recognizing that conventional military methods of defense were no longer applicable.

George Leader believed in a strong national defense system. During his administration, he supported measures to maintain the National Guard. Some federal officials would have liked to weaken or even eliminate the Guard in favor of the Reserve. Leader continually stressed the need for the Guard both in times of state emergency and as a reserve force for the nation. He believed that there was no contradiction in maintaining a strong Guard and a strong Reserve because for him the civilian soldier provided the best defense. As a permanent member of the community, the civilian soldiers of the Guard and Reserve were more committed to the defense and well-being of the community than the professional soldier.

There were two branches of the Pennsylvania National Guard: Army and Air. The Army, commanded by Colonel Richard Snyder, had conventional infantry, artillery, engineering units. The Air National Guard, commanded by Colonel Richard Posey, was equipped with jet aircraft for air defense. During the Leader administration a new Air Transportation Squadron was added to the Pennsylvania Air National Guard at Reading; it provided another defense for the state in times of attack or emergency.

The Guard's peacetime value was exhibited during the floods that followed the hurricanes in 1955. The Guard provided manpower, transportation, and property protection. Since 1,800 guardsmen were in training at Indiantown Gap at the time, they were immediately available, and the state did not even have to pay for their mobilization, since the troops were being paid by the federal training funds.

THE STATE COUNCIL OF CIVIL DEFENSE

The State Council of Civil Defense was a group of citizens responsible for developing civil defense plans and coordinating volunteers. The council's activities were run by the Director, Dr. Richard Gerstell.

The Leader administration years followed the Second World War and coincided with the end of the Korean Conflict. The nation's cold war policies and the threat of nuclear attack were on many people's minds. Governor Leader, consistent with his belief in a strong national defense, was concerned about the well-being of the citizens and worried whether they were prepared for a national emergency. Leader said, "People can no longer afford the perilous luxury of paying no heed to the fact that we are now wide open to atomic attack." He often repeated that this was everyone's problem, not just that of those who lived in more populated areas. Pittsburgh and Philadelphia were natural targets, but so were other small cities in the state; fallout would affect everyone. Besides self-protection, people had to be ready to help others. The citizens in the rural areas had to be ready to help the evacuees of the larger cities, and Pennsylvania had to be prepared to assist neighboring states if the need arose.

Numerous state-wide tests of the emergency broadcasting system, the adequacy of evacuation plans, and the state of emergency equipment were made. The Governor sent a group of citizens to New York to study its civil defense system, considered one of the best in the nation. Leader hoped that Pennsylvania could develop a system comparable to that in New York State.

Civil defense units around the country were aided by the passage of two federal bills, one allowing the federal government to help state civil defense organizations by providing funds for those units, and one authorizing the state civil defense units to purchase surplus equipment.

Perhaps a militia is more significant historically and sentimentally to a Commonwealth of colonial origin. Certainly Leader's devotion to the Guard, though tempered with practical motivations, was deeply historical. His insistence on high calibre leadership and his attempts to clarify state and federal relationships and responsibilities are consistent with his other applications of good administrative policy.

STATE POLICE

The Pennsylvania State Police, founded in 1905, was the first state police force in the nation. It had a long and proud tradition of excellence and became a model for other states. The duties of the 1,900 officers included highway patrol, criminal investigation, and enforcement of state laws. During Leader's administration the state police conducted a number of important investigations in conjunction with the

203

Department of Justice. Among them were the investigations of the Turnpike Commission and the Delaware Bridge Commission. One of the other duties of the state police was to drive the governor's car and protect the chief executive.

At the beginning of his administration, George Leader had not yet selected a State Police Commissioner. Colonel Wilhelm had been commissioner for twelve years and at age 73 was ready to retire. Wilhelm was the last of the original officers recruited in 1905. The Democratic party leaders suggested Major Earl J. Henry, the officer in charge of the Traffic Bureau, as a possible candidate even though he was a Republican. In March 1955, Governor Leader appointed Henry to the post, because he was competent and popular with the enlisted men.

Henry's first problem was filling the position of Deputy Commissioner. He preferred Captain Dahlstrom but the Democrats wanted Frank McCartney to receive the appointment. Although McCartney had an outstanding record as a sergeant in the Investigating Bureau, he was not a commissioned officer. Henry was convinced that the morale of the state police force would suffer if leadership was not restricted to the commissioned officers. Henry resisted the party's pressure and Dahlstrom became the Deputy Commissioner.

The state police had always been a separate entity in state government, but Leader's Office of Administration changed that somewhat. The police force did not welcome what it feared would be unwanted intervention by the Office of Administration. The management programs of the Office of Administration did affect the state police in a number of areas. Job reclassification was completed and the name "trooper" was officially adopted in this reclassification. The term "trooper" had been the popular name for the private in the state police force. Most of the ranking officers did not favor the name change, but Lieutenant Nevin was able to have the idea accepted by the Office of Administration. This office also discovered that there was little difference in financial rewards for promotion into higher ranks. The Office of Administration authorized new pay increments which provided larger increases in the higher positions but little or nothing for promotion within the lower ranks. This and the new policy of promotion, which included consideration of seniority, increased the morale problem.

Colonel Henry faced a difficult problem with morale during his tenure as Commissioner. Like Commissioners before him, he had to contend with poor morale among the ranks of enlisted men who saw only a few of their own numbers rise to leadership positions. George Leader called this one of the administration's most difficult employee problems, so a number of programs were tried to improve the morale of the state police. Among them were equipment improvements like new patrol cars to ensure the safety of the officers on the highway, and new uniforms. The new summer uniforms were introduced to make the troopers more comfortable in hot weather and cold weather gear was improved to protect them in foul weather. But these improvements in equipment did not really affect the real source of the morale problem which was the lack of sufficient career advancement opportunities.

The State Police Training School located in Hershey was outdated. Surveys for a new site could not identify another feasible spot in Hershey, so planners looked elsewhere for a location of a new school. When individuals at the Hershey Estates heard that the State Police were planning to relocate because of high land prices, they offered to sell the state twenty-eight acres of land for one dollar. The State Police School was a tourist attraction in Hershey and they wanted to keep it. Construction on the new school began in Hershey in 1958.

One other notable addition to the State Police duties was the installation of the National Warning System. The State Police agreed to man this system, which belonged to the state Civil Defense System, in exchange for the right to use it in times of emergency.

The Later Years

George Leader was confident that the Democratic party was strong enough in 1959 to elect him to the U.S. Senate as the Pennsylvania Republicans had done for a number of governors before him. But that was not to be the case. Despite the Democrats winning a majority in both houses and electing Governor Lawrence in 1959, George Leader lost to Republican Hugh Scott in the U.S. Senate race. It is debatable whether Leader's loss can be attributed to the public's dislike for increased sales tax, to the Democratic county chairmen's displeasure with the loss of patronage jobs, or to some other factors. Whatever the cause, the loss discouraged Leader from running for public office again. This did not mean that George Leader remained outside of politics. He stayed active in the state and national scene. Leader was a delegate to the Democratic National conventions a number of times; he worked for the election of Governor Shapp, and local Democrats often sought his endorsement. State Democratic leaders approached him several times to run again for governor, but he always declined. Leader's reluctance to accept another nomination for governor stemmed from his previous defeat for the U.S. Senate. He felt this indicated that he would not have enough party support to win; and, by this time, he was totally committed to his business endeavors.

After he left office, George Leader remained active in state government through his participation in a number of bipartisan committees. These committees included three for revision of Pennsylvania's constitution. A number of governors, including Leader, had attempted to achieve a revision of the state constitution, but it was not until Governor Shafer's administration that the Constitution Convention was convened. Governor Shafer requested former Governors Leader and Scranton to co-chair a committee for revising the constitution and two subsequent committees which worked for passage of the constitutional amendments. They shared the chairmanship of a number of bipartisan committees in other administrations, one which worked to reduce the real estate taxes on farmland, and two committees which supported changes in banking legislation.

Leader was also a candidate for a number of administrative positions in the state and federal governments. For example Governor Lawrence offered Leader the position of Secretary of Public Welfare, which Leader declined. He explained that his administration had made great strides in forming and modernizing the state's welfare department and mental health system; and he did not want to head a department which would be affected by Lawrence's determination to cut spending, resulting in a loss of financial and administrative support. In addition, he had served four years as governor and made decisions concerning the entire Commonwealth, so he did not think he would be content running only a small part of state government.

When George Leader left the office of governor, he accepted a job as a mortgage banker in Philadelphia. Although he was not directly involved in the activities of state government, his status as former governor provided him with many contacts and activities in fields outside of banking.

The governor remained very interested in both the physical and mental health fields. As chairman of Pennsylvania's Senior Citizens for John F. Kennedy, Leader spoke often about Medicare during the 1960 presidential campaign. He was active in the American Cancer Society and in 1967 he served as the chairman for the state fund raising campaign; two years later he served as its national fund-raising chairman. He was also a member of several boards of trustees, including two with medical schools: Temple University and Hahnemann Medical College. These positions kept the former governor informed on activities and developments in the medical field, and the care of institutionalized citizens, which had such a profound affect on him during his administration, remained in his mind. He was sure that there had to be a better way of caring for the handicapped, mentally ill, and the elderly.

In 1959, while in Oregon, George Leader visited nursing homes operated by Hillhaven, probably the most progressive nursing homes in the country at that time. Leader was impressed with their methods of operations, and subsequently visited more of the homes in California when he attended the Democratic National Convention in Los Angeles. Seeing that a way of providing decent care for the elderly existed, he was convinced that this aspect of the health care field interested him the most. Discussions with the Hillhaven management produced an offer; Leader would open a group of nursing homes as part of the chain on the East Coast. When he came back to Philadelphia, his bankers were not impressed with his proposal to open a chain of nursing homes, questioning how anyone could make money caring for the elderly. Although discouraged, Leader was convinced that he could run a profitable business providing quality care for the elderly. He was sure that the private sector could help the needy receive the best health care possible by using good management methods. A few years later he and an associate purchased a nursing home in Yeadon. Subsequently, he established the Leader Nursing and Rehabilitation Centers and now has more than 20 centers in Pennsylvania.

George Leader is known not only for his use of public administration in state government and the promotion of human service programs, but also his consistency. The beliefs he espoused as governor continue to characterize his life as private citizen and businessman. He still maintains the same beliefs about hard work, fair play, good staff, adequate information, sound business procedures, conservation, and humanitarian service.

George Leader believes that honest, fair, hard working, and consistent people will be successful. He proved this as governor and he continues to prove it as a private citizen.

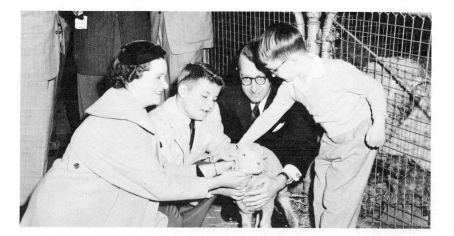

Index